BACON

Portraits and Self-Portraits

BACON

Portraits and Self-Portraits

introduction by
Milan Kundera

France Borel

THAMES AND HUDSON

Translated from the French *Bacon: Portraits et autoportraits*
by Ruth Taylor (text by France Borel and Chronology)
and Linda Asher (text by Milan Kundera)

First published in Great Britain in 1996 by Thames and Hudson Ltd, London

First published in the United States of America in 1996
by Thames and Hudson Inc., 500 Fifth Avenue, New York, New York 10110

Library of Congress Catalog Card Number 96-61101

British Library Cataloguing-in-Publication Data
A catalogue record for this book is available from the British Library

ISBN 0-500-09266-4

Printed and bound in France

CONTENTS

The Painter's Brutal Gesture   *Milan Kundera*
8

Portraits and Self-Portraits
20

Francis Bacon: The Face Flayed   *France Borel*
187

Chronology
205

One-man Exhibitions
208

Filmography
210

Bibliography
211

List of Works
212

Acknowledgments
216

MILAN KUNDERA

The Painter's Brutal Gesture

When Michel Archimbaud was planning this collection of Francis Bacon's portraits and self-portraits, he asked me to write the book's introduction. He assured me that the invitation was Bacon's own wish. He reminded me of a short piece of mine, published long ago in the periodical *L'Arc*, a piece he said the painter had considered one of the few in which he could recognize himself. I will not deny my emotion at this message arriving, after years, from an artist I had never met and loved so much.

That piece in *L'Arc* (which later inspired a section of my *Book of Laughter and Forgetting*), discussing the triptych of the portraits of Henrietta Moraes, was written in about 1977, in the very first period after my emigration, obsessed as I was then by recollections of the country which I had just left and which still remained in my memory as the land of interrogations and surveillance. Here it is:

2

It was 1972. I met with a girl in a Prague suburb, in a borrowed apartment. Two days earlier, she had been interrogated by the police about me for an entire day. Now she wanted to meet with me secretly (she feared that she was constantly being followed) to tell me what questions they had asked her and how she had answered them. If they were to interrogate me, my answers should be the same as hers.

She was a very young girl who had as yet little experience of the world. The interrogation had disturbed her, and, after three days, the fear was still upsetting her bowels. She was very pale and during our conversation she kept leaving the room to go to the toilet — so that our whole encounter was accompanied by the noise of the water refilling the tank.

I had known her for a long time. She was intelligent, spirited, she had fine emotional control, and was always so impeccably dressed that her outfit, just like her behaviour, allowed not a hint of nakedness. And now, suddenly, fear like a great knife had laid her open. She was gaping wide before me like the split carcass of a heifer hanging from a meat hook.

The noise of the water refilling the toilet tank practically never let up, and I suddenly had the urge to rape her. I know what I'm saying: rape her, not make love to her. I didn't want tenderness from her. I wanted to bring my hand down brutally on her face and in one swift instant take her completely, with all her unbearably arousing contradictions: with her impeccable outfit along with her rebellious guts, her good sense along with her fear, her pride along with her misery. I sensed that all those contradictions harboured her essence: that treasure, that nugget of gold, that diamond hidden in the depths. I wanted to possess her, in one swift moment, with her shit along with her ineffable soul.

But I saw those two eyes staring at me, filled with torment (two tormented eyes in a sensible face) and the more tormented those eyes, the more my desire turned absurd, stupid, scandalous, incomprehensible and impossible to carry out.

Uncalled-for and unconscionable, that desire was nonetheless real. I cannot disavow it – and when I look at Francis Bacon's portrait-triptych, it's as if I recall it. The painter's gaze comes down on the face like a brutal hand trying to seize hold of her essence, of that diamond hidden in the depths. Of course we are not certain that the depths really do harbour something – but whatever it may be, we each of us have in us that brutal gesture, that hand movement that roughs up another person's face in the hope of finding, in it and behind it, a thing that is hidden there.

3

The best commentaries on Bacon's work are by Bacon himself in two series of interviews: with David Sylvester between 1962 and 1975 and published in the latter year, and with Archimbaud between October 1991 and April 1992. In both he speaks admiringly of Picasso, especially of the 1926–1932 period, the only one to which he feels truly close; he saw 'an area there…which in a way has been unexplored, of organic form that relates to the human image but is a complete distortion of it'. With this very precise remark, he defines the realm whose exploration is actually his alone.

Aside from that short period Bacon mentions, one could say that Picasso's *light gesture* transforms human body motifs into *two-dimensional* and autonomous pictorial reality. With Bacon we are in another world: there, playful Picassian (or Matissian) euphoria is replaced by an amazement (if not a shock) at what we are, what we are materially, physically. Impelled by that amazement, the painter's hand (to use the words of my old piece) comes down with a 'brutal gesture' on a body, on a face, 'in the hope of finding, in it and behind it, a thing that is hidden there'.

But what is hidden there? Its self? Every portrait ever painted seeks to uncover the subject's self. But Bacon lived in a time when the self inevitably eludes detection. Indeed, our most common personal experience teaches us (especially if the life behind us is very long) that faces are lamentably alike (the insane demographic avalanche further enhancing that sense), that they are easy to confuse, that they only differ one from the next by some very tiny, barely perceptible detail, which mathematically often represents only a few millimetres' difference in the various proportions. Add to that our historical experience, which teaches us that men mimic one another, that their attitudes are statistically calculable, their opinions manipulable, and that man is therefore less an individual than an element of a mass.

This is the moment of uncertainty when the rapist hand of the painter comes down with a 'brutal gesture' on his subjects' faces in order to find, somewhere in the depths, their buried self. What is new in that Baconian quest is, first (to use his expression), the 'organic' nature of those forms in 'a complete distortion'. Which means that the forms in his paintings are meant to resemble living beings, to recall their bodily existence, their flesh, and thus always to retain their *three-dimensional* nature. The second innovation is the principle of variations. Edmund Husserl explained the importance of variations for searching out the essence of a phenomenon. I will say it in my simpler way: variations differ one from the other, but yet retain some thing common to them all; the thing they have in common is 'that treasure, that nugget of gold, that hidden diamond', namely, the sought-for essence of a theme or, in Bacon's case, the self of a face.

Looking at Bacon's portraits, I am amazed that, despite their 'distortion', they all look like their subject. But how can an image look like a subject of which it is consciously, programmatically, a distortion? And yet it does look like the subject; photos of the persons portrayed bear that out; and even if I did not know those photos, it is clear that in all the series, in all the triptychs, the various deformations of the face resemble one another, so that one recognizes in them some one and the same person. However 'distorted', these portraits are *faithful*. That is what I find miraculous.

4

I could put it differently: Bacon's portraits are the interrogation on the *limits* of the self. Up to what degree of distortion does an individual still remain himself? To what degree of distortion does a beloved being still remain a beloved being? For how long does a cherished face growing remote through illness, through madness, through hatred, through death still remain recognizable? Where lies the border beyond which a self ceases to be a self?

5

For a long time, Bacon and Beckett made up a couple in my imaginary gallery of modern art. Then I read the Archimbaud interview: 'I've always been amazed by this pairing of Beckett and me', Bacon said. Then, farther on: '...I've always felt that Shakespeare expressed much better and more precisely and more powerfully what Beckett and Joyce were trying to say...'. And again: 'I wonder if Beckett's ideas about his art haven't wound up killing off his creation. There's something at once too systematic and too intelligent in him, that may be what's always bothered me.' And finally: 'In painting, we always leave in too much that is habit, we never eliminate enough, but in Beckett I've often had the sense that as a result of seeking to eliminate, nothing was left any more, and that nothingness finally sounded hollow...'.

When one artist talks about another one, he is always talking (indirectly, in a roundabout way) of himself, and that is what's valuable in his judgment. In talking about Beckett, what is Bacon telling us about himself?

That he is refusing to be categorized. That he wants to protect his work against clichés.

Next: that he is resisting the dogmatists of modernism who have erected a barrier between tradition and modern art as if, in the history of art, the latter represented an isolated period with its own incomparable values, with its completely autonomous criteria. Whereas Bacon looks to the history of art in its entirety; the twentieth century does not cancel our debts to Shakespeare.

And further: he is refusing to express his ideas on art in too systematic a fashion, fearing to stifle his creative unconscious; fearing also to allow his art to be turned into a kind of simplistic message. He knows that the danger is all the greater because, in our half of the century, art is clogged with a noisy, opaque logorrhoea of theory that prevents a work from coming into direct, media-free contact with its viewer (its reader, its listener).

Wherever he can, Bacon therefore blurs his tracks to throw off interpreters who try to reduce his work to an over-facile programme: he bridles at using the word 'horror' with regard to his art; he stresses the role of chance in his painting (chance turning up in the course of the work – an accidental spot of paint that abruptly changes the very subject of the picture); he insists on the word 'play' when everyone is making much of the seriousness of his paintings. People want to talk about his despair? Very well, but, he specifies immediately, in this case it is a *joyous despair*.

6

From the reflection on Beckett quoted, I pull out this remark: 'In painting, we always leave in too much that is habit, we never eliminate enough...'. Too much that is habit, which is to say: everything in painting that is not the painter's own discovery, his fresh contribution, his originality; everything that is inherited, routine, filler, elaboration considered to be technical necessity. That describes, for example, in the sonata form (of even the greatest – Mozart, Beethoven) all the (often very conventional) transitions from one theme to another. Almost all great modern artists mean to do away with 'filler', do away with whatever comes from habit, from technical routine, whatever keeps them from getting directly and exclusively at the essential (the essential: the thing the artist himself, and only he, is able to say).

So it is with Bacon: the backgrounds of his paintings are hyper-simple, flat-colour; but: in the foreground, the bodies are treated with a richness of colours and forms that is all the denser. Now, that (Shakespearian) richness is what matters to him. For without that richness (richness contrasting with the flat-colour background), the beauty would be ascetic, as if 'put on a diet', as if diminished, and for Bacon the issue always and above all is beauty, the explosion of beauty, because even if the word seems nowadays to be hackneyed, out of date, it is what links him to Shakespeare.

And it is why he is irritated by the word 'horror' that is persistently applied to his painting. Tolstoy said of Leonid Andreyev and of his tales of terror: 'He's trying to frighten me, but I'm not scared.' Nowadays there are too many paintings trying to frighten us, and they annoy us instead. Terror is not an aesthetic sensation, and the horror found in Tolstoy's novels is never there to frighten us; the harrowing scene in which they operate on the mortally wounded Andrei Bolkonsky without anaesthesia is not lacking in beauty; as no scene in Shakespeare lacks it; as no picture by Bacon lacks it. Butchers' shops are horrible, but speaking of them, Bacon says, 'one has got to remember as a painter that there is this great beauty of the colour of meat.'

Why is it that, despite all Bacon's reservations, I continue to see him as akin to Beckett?

Both of them are located at just about the same place in the respective histories of their art. That is, in the very last period of dramatic art, in the very last period of the history of painting. For Bacon is one of the last painters whose language is still oil and brush. And Beckett still wrote for the theatre that was based on the author's text. After him, the theatre still exists, true, perhaps it is even evolving; but it is no longer the playwrights' texts that inspire, renew, guarantee that evolution.

In the history of modern art, Bacon and Beckett are not the ones opening the way; they close it again. When Archimbaud asks Bacon which contemporary painters are important to him, he says: 'After Picasso, I don't know. There's a pop-art show at the Royal Academy right now...when you see all those paintings together, you don't see anything. To me there's nothing in it, it's empty, completely empty.' And Warhol? '...to me, he's not important'. And abstract art? Oh no, he doesn't like it.

'After Picasso, I don't know.' He talks like an orphan. And he is one. He is one even in the very concrete sense of the life he lived: the people who opened the way were surrounded by colleagues, by commentators, by worshippers, by sympathizers, by fellow travellers, by an entire gang. But Bacon is alone. As Beckett is. In one of the Sylvester interviews: 'I think it would be more exciting to be one of a number of artists working together.... I think it would be terribly nice to have someone to talk to. Today there is absolutely no one to talk to.'

Because their modernism, the modernism that closes the way again, no longer matches the 'modernity' around them, a *modernity of fashions* propelled by the marketing of art. (Sylvester: 'If abstract paintings are no more than pattern-making, how do you explain the fact that there are people like myself who have the same sort of visceral response to them at times as they have to figurative works?' Bacon: 'Fashion.') Being modern at the moment when the great modernism is closing the way is an entirely different thing from being modern in Picasso's time. Bacon is isolated ('there is absolutely no one to talk to'); isolated from both the past and the future.

8

Like Bacon, Beckett had no illusions about the future either of the world or of art. And at that moment in the last days of illusions, both men show the same immensely interesting and significant reaction: wars, revolutions and their setbacks, massacres, the imposture we call democracy – all these subjects are absent from their works. In his *Rhinoceros*, Ionesco is still interested in the great political questions. Nothing like that in Beckett. Picasso paints *Massacre in Korea*. An inconceivable subject for Bacon. Living through the end of a civilization (as Beckett and Bacon were or thought they were), the ultimate brutal confrontation is not with a society, with a state, with a politics, but with the physiological materiality of man. That is why even the great subject of the Crucifixion, which used to concentrate within itself the whole ethics, the whole religion, indeed the whole history of the West, becomes in Bacon's hands a simple physiological scandal. 'I've always been very moved by pictures about slaughterhouses and meat, and to me they belong very much to the whole thing of the Crucifixion. There've been extraordinary photographs which have been done of animals just being taken up before they were slaughtered; and the smell of death...'.

To link Jesus nailed to the Cross with slaughterhouses and animals' fear might seem sacrilegious. But Bacon is a non-believer, and the notion of sacrilege has no place in his way of thinking; according to him, 'man now realizes that he is an accident, that he is a completely futile being, that he has to play out the game without reason.' Seen from that angle, Jesus is that accident who, without reason, played out the game. The Cross: the game played to the end.

No, not sacrilege; rather a clear-sighted, sorrowing, thoughtful gaze that tries to penetrate into the essential. And what essential thing is revealed when all the social dreams have evaporated and man sees 'religious possibilities...completely cancelled out for him'? The body. The mere *Ecce homo*, visible, moving, and concrete. For 'of course we are meat, we are potential carcasses. If I go into a butcher's shop I always think it's surprising that I wasn't there instead of the animal.'

It is neither pessimism nor despair, it is only obvious fact, but a fact that is veiled by our membership in a collectivity that blinds us with its dreams, its excitements, its projects, its illusions, its struggles, its causes, its religions, its ideologies, its passions. And then one day the veil falls and we are left stranded with the body, at the body's mercy, like the young woman in Prague who, following the shock of an interrogation, went off to the toilet every three minutes. She was reduced to her fear, to the fury of her bowels, and to the noise of the water she heard refilling the toilet tank as I hear it when I look at Bacon's *Figure at a Washbasin* of 1976 or the *Triptych May–June 1973*. For that young Prague woman it was no longer the police that she had to face up to but her own belly, and if someone was presiding invisibly over that little horror scene, it was no policeman, or apparatchik, or executioner, it was a God – or an anti-God, the wicked God of the Gnostics, a Demiurge, a Creator, the one who had trapped us for ever by that 'accident' of the body he cobbled together in his workshop and of which, for a while, we are forced to become the soul.

Bacon often spied on that workshop of the Creator; it can be seen, for instance, in the pictures called *Studies of the Human Body*, in which he unmasks the body as a simple 'accident', an accident that could as easily have been fashioned some other way, for instance – I don't know – with three hands, or with the eyes set in the knees. These are the only pictures of his that fill me with horror. But is 'horror' the right word? No. For the sensation that these pictures arouse, there is no right word. What they arouse is not the horror we know, the one in response to the insanities of history, to torture, persecution, war, massacres, suffering. No. This is a different horror: it comes from the *accidental nature*, suddenly unveiled by the painter, of the human body.

9

What is left to us when we have come down to that?

The face;

the face that harbours 'that treasure, that nugget of gold, that hidden diamond' which is the infinitely fragile self shivering in a body;

the face I gaze upon to seek in it a reason for living the 'completely futile accident' that is life.

Translated from the French by Linda Asher

Portrait
c.1931–1932
Pastel on paper
40 x 32 cm

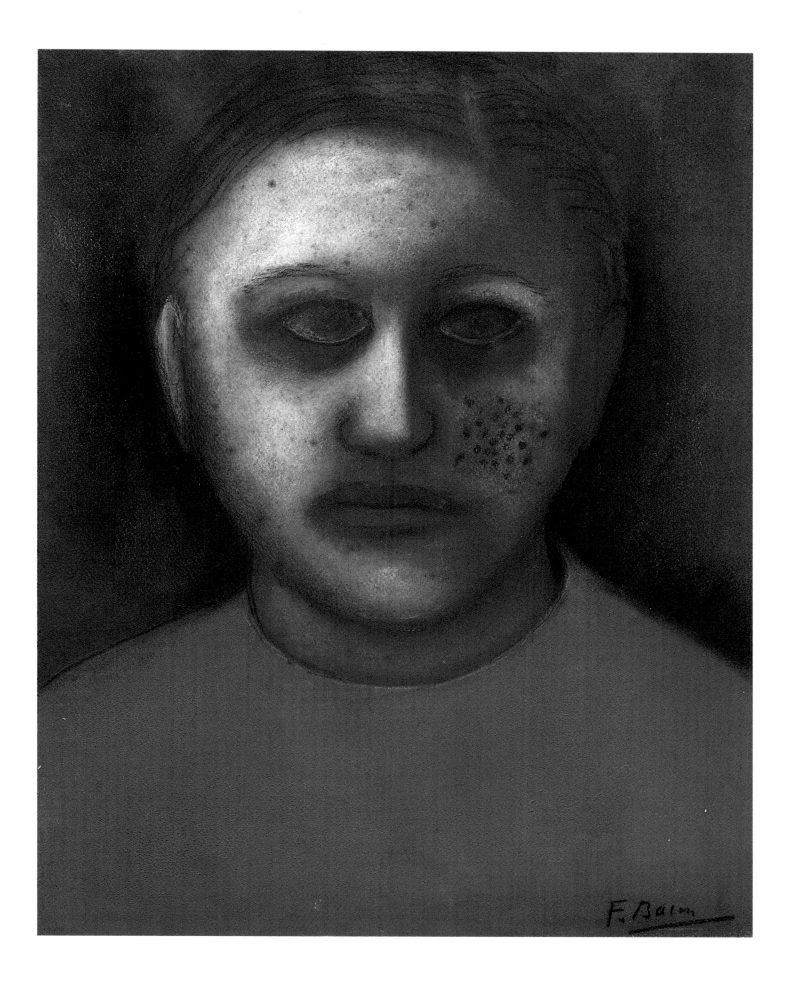

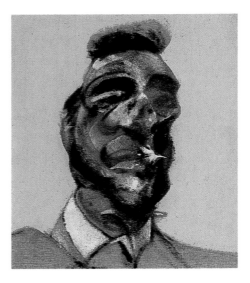
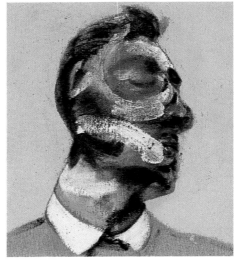
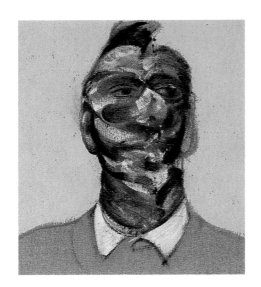

Three Studies for
Portrait of George Dyer
(on light ground)
1964
Oil on canvas
35.5 x 30.5 cm (each)

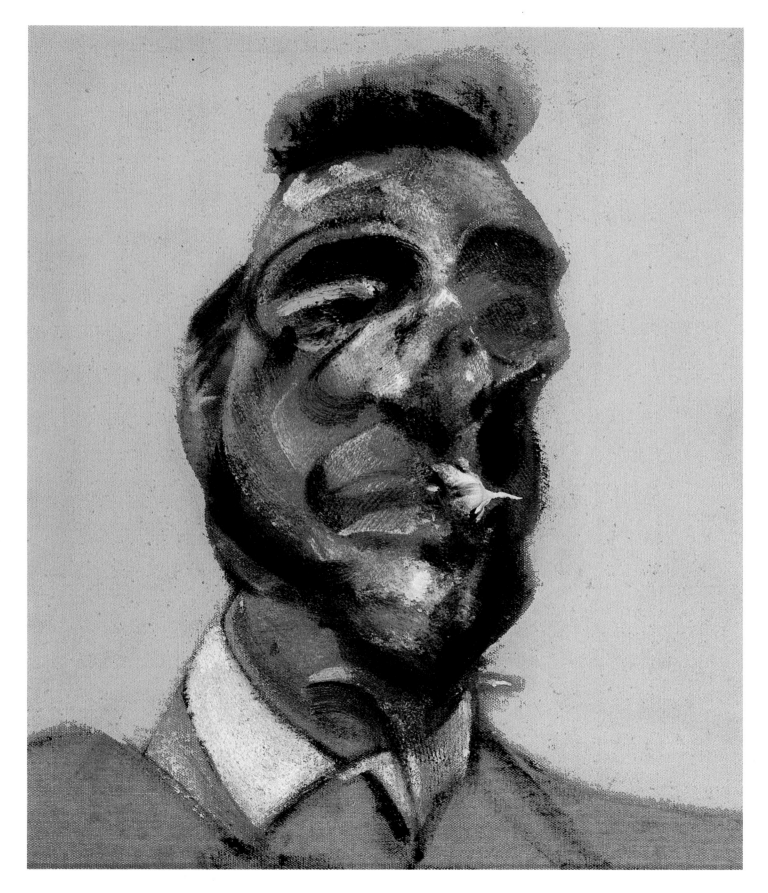

24

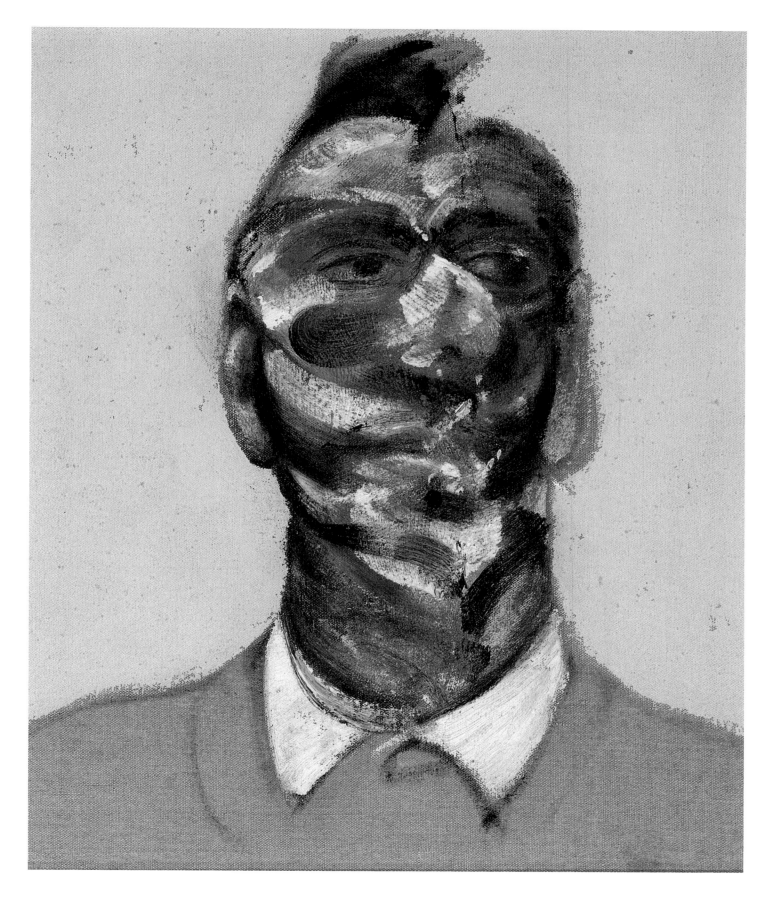

Study for Head of George Dyer 1967

26   Oil on canvas 35.5 x 30.5 cm

Self-Portrait 1972

Oil on canvas 35.5 x 30.5 cm

 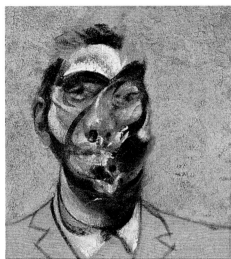 

Three Studies for
Portrait of George Dyer
(on pink ground)
1964
Oil on canvas
35.5 x 30.5 cm (each)

Self-Portrait 1972

Oil on canvas 35.5 x 30.5 cm

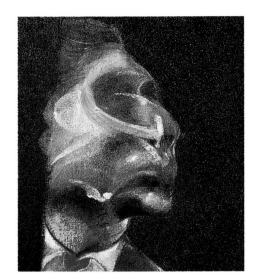  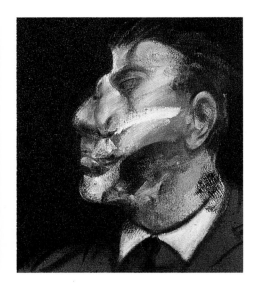

Three Studies of George Dyer
1966
Oil on canvas
35.5 x 30.5 cm (each)
(opposite: detail)

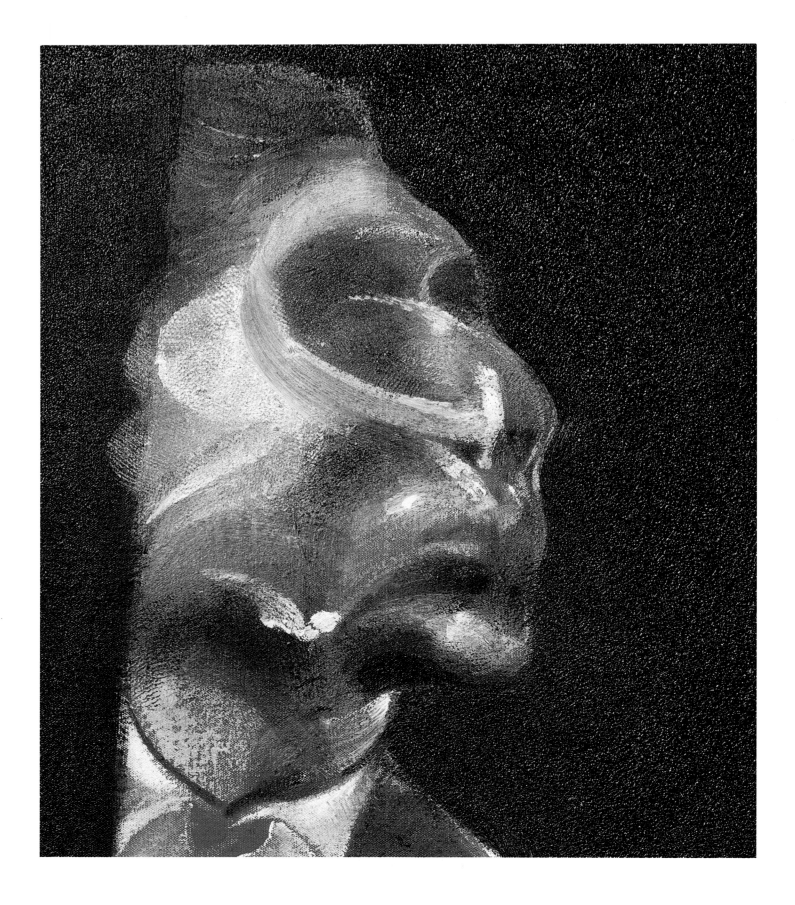

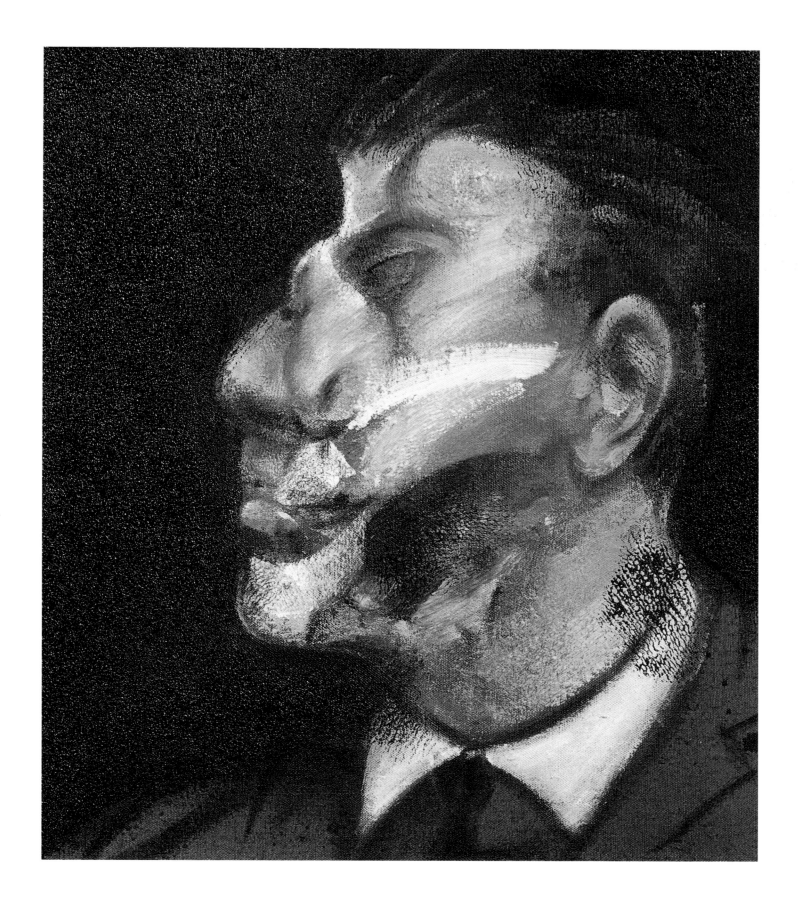

Three Studies for Portrait of
Isabel Rawsthorne
1965
Oil on canvas
35.5 x 30.5 cm (each)
(opposite: detail)

38

Three Studies of Isabel Rawsthorne
(on white ground)
1965
Oil on canvas
35.5 x 30.5 cm (each)

Study for Self-Portrait 1973
Oil on canvas
35.5 x 30.5 cm
(opposite)

41

42

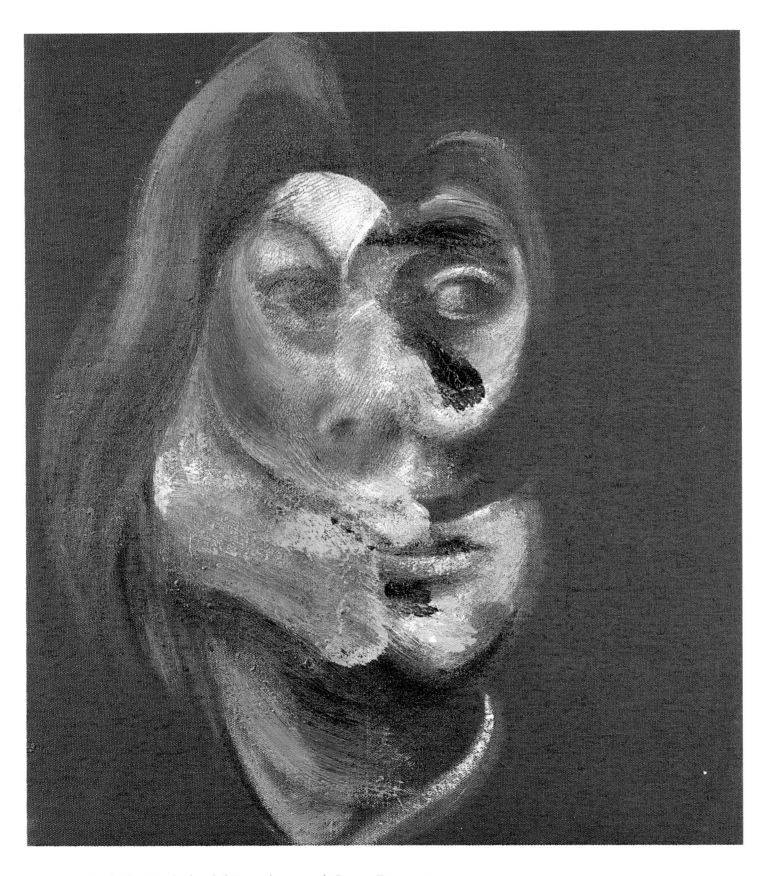

Study for Head of Isabel Rawsthorne and George Dyer 1967

44   Oil on canvas 35.5 x 30.5 cm (each)

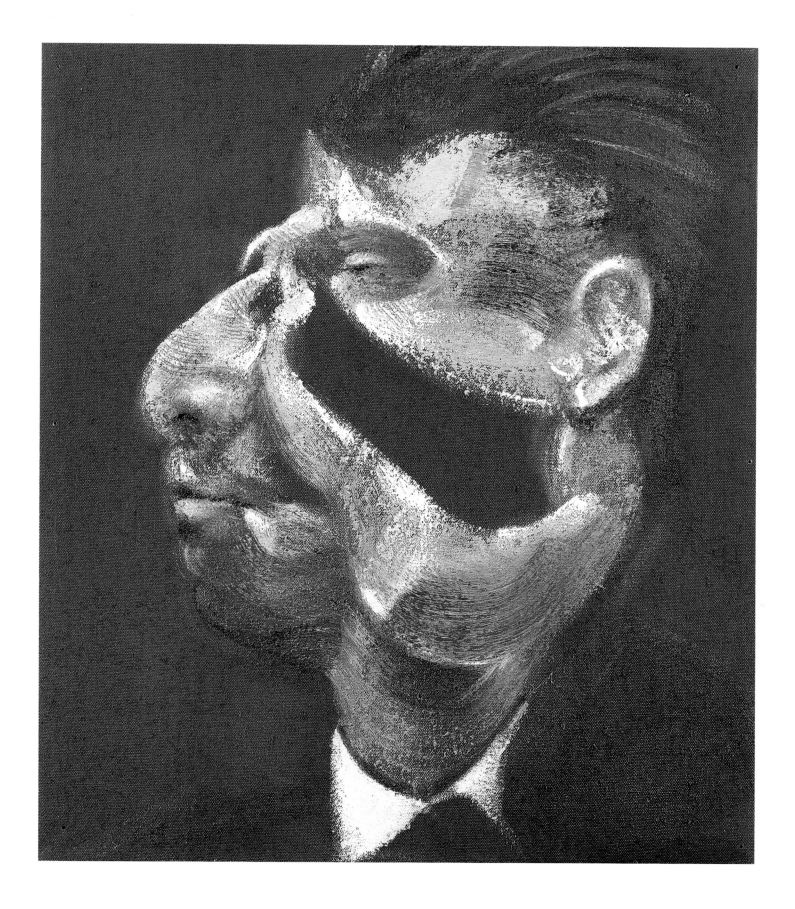

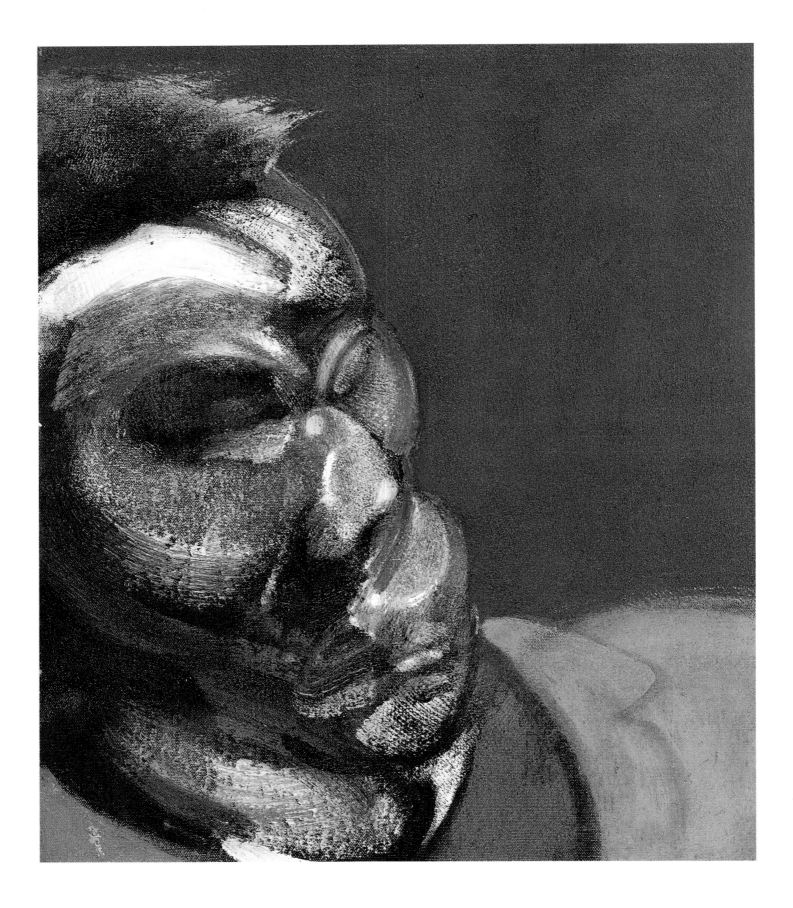

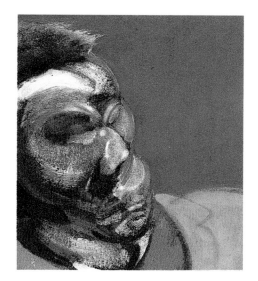 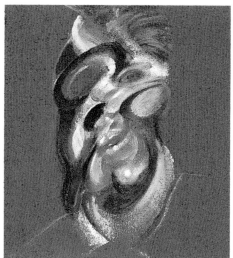 

Three Studies for a
Self-Portrait
1967
Oil on canvas
35.5 x 30.5 cm (each)

49

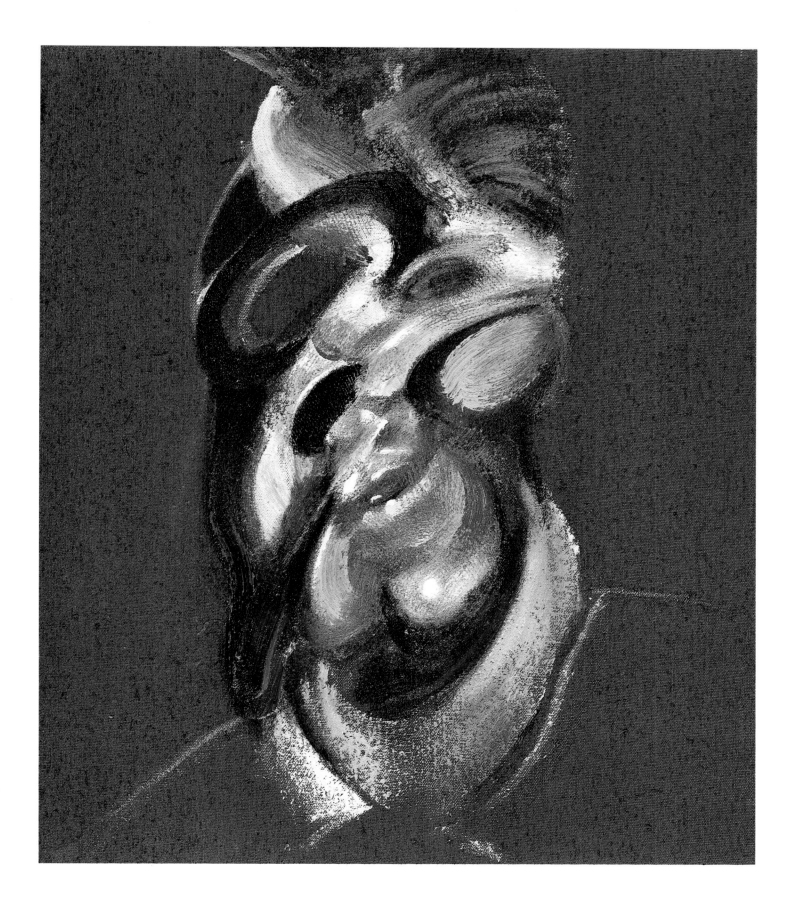

47

Study for Head of Isabel Rawsthorne 1967

Oil on canvas 35.5 x 30.5 cm

Three Studies of Isabel Rawsthorne
1968
Oil on canvas
35.5 x 30.5 cm (each)

*Studies of George Dyer and
Isabel Rawsthorne*
1970
Oil on canvas
35.5 x 30.5 cm (each)

Study of Isabel Rawsthorne 1966
Oil on canvas
35.5 x 30.5 cm
(opposite)

*Four Studies
for a Self-Portrait*
1967
Oil on canvas
91.5 x 33 cm
(opposite and page 60: details)

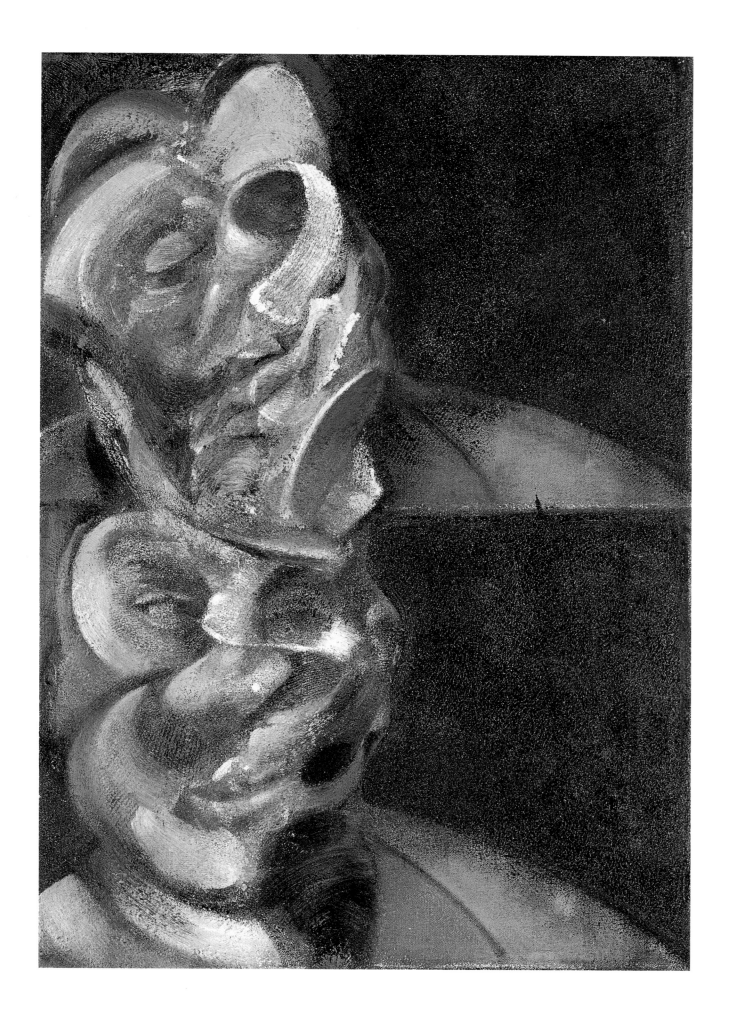

Self-Portrait 1975

Oil on canvas 35.5 x 30.5 cm (opposite)

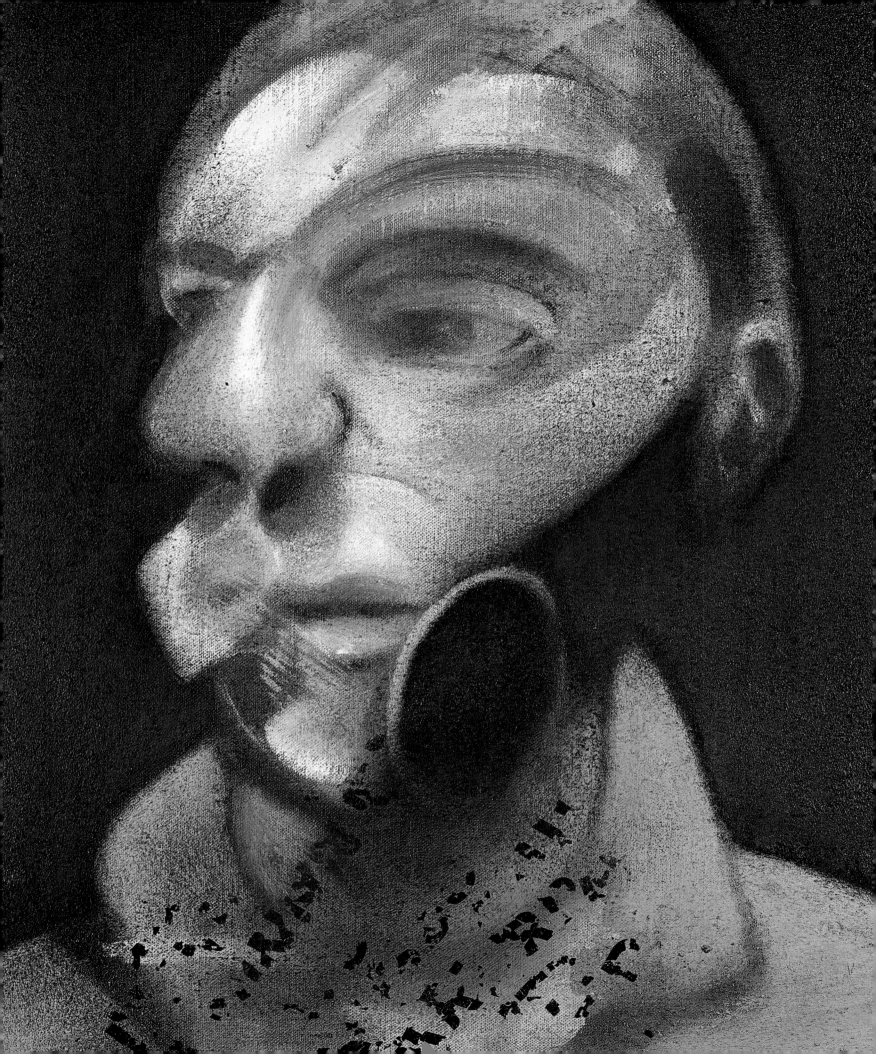

Study for Head of Isabel Rawsthorne 1967

Oil on canvas 35.5 x 30.5 cm

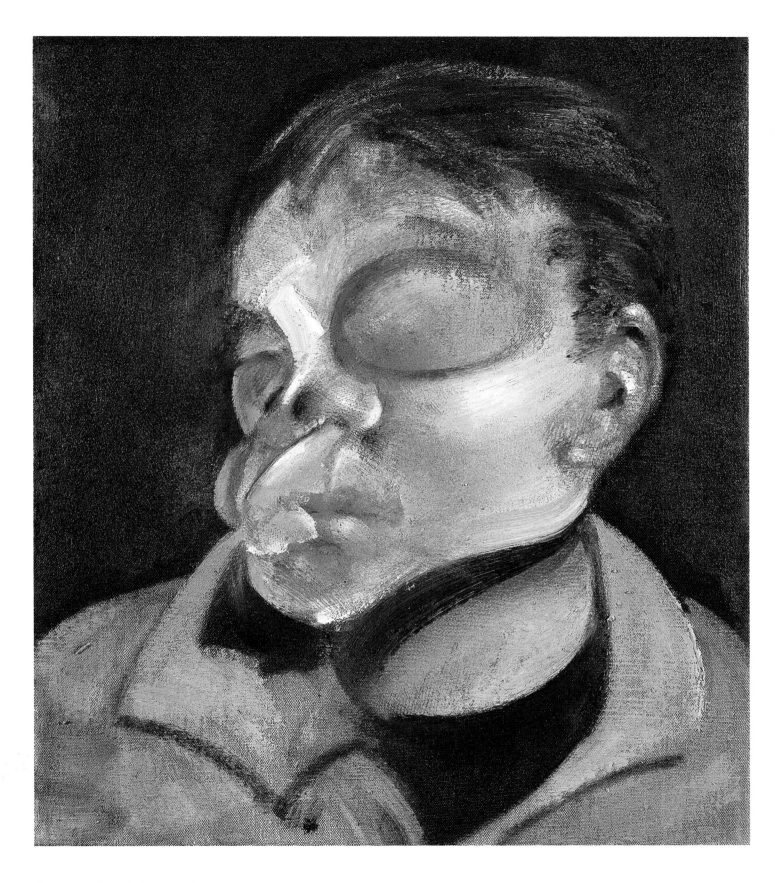

Self-Portrait with Injured Eye 1972
Oil on canvas 35.5 x 30.5 cm

Three Studies for Self-Portrait
1972
Oil on canvas
35.5 x 30.5 cm (each)
(opposite: detail)

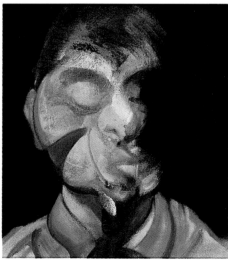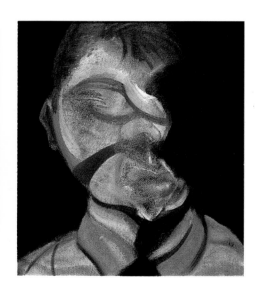

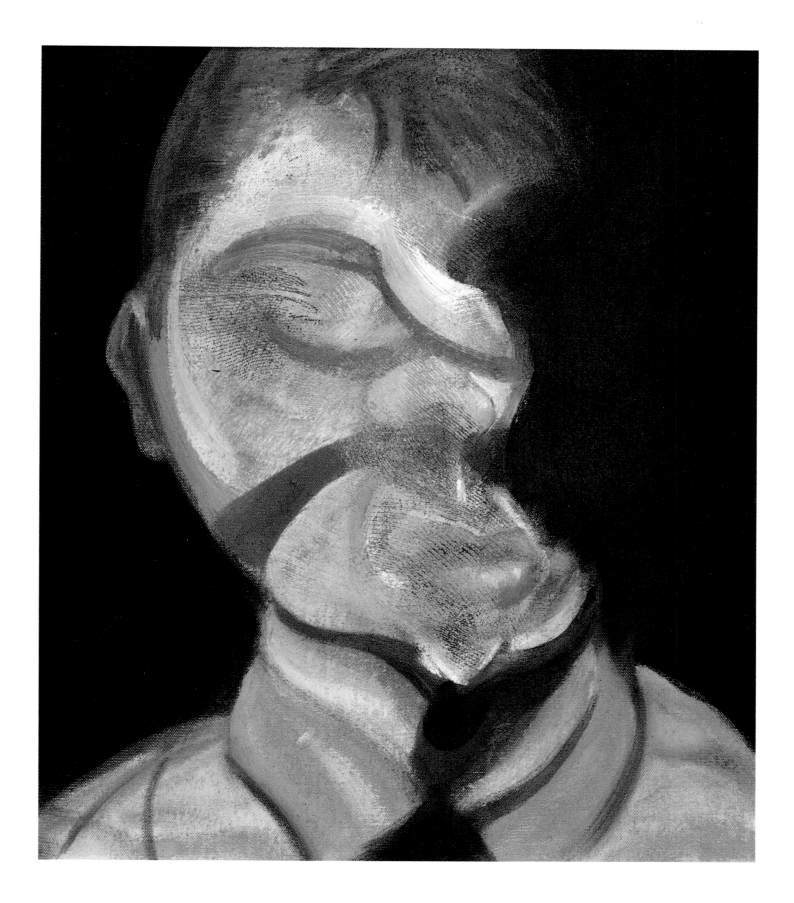

70

Three Studies of
Isabel Rawsthorne
(on light ground)
1965
Oil on canvas
35.5 x 30.5 cm (each)

Three Studies of
Isabel Rawsthorne
1966
Oil on canvas
35.5 x 30.5 cm (each)
(opposite: detail)

  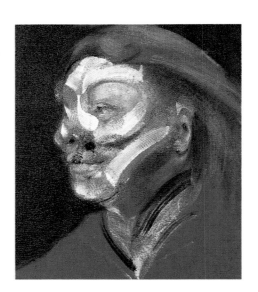

Two Studies for Self-Portrait 1977
Oil on canvas 35.5 x 30.5 cm (each)

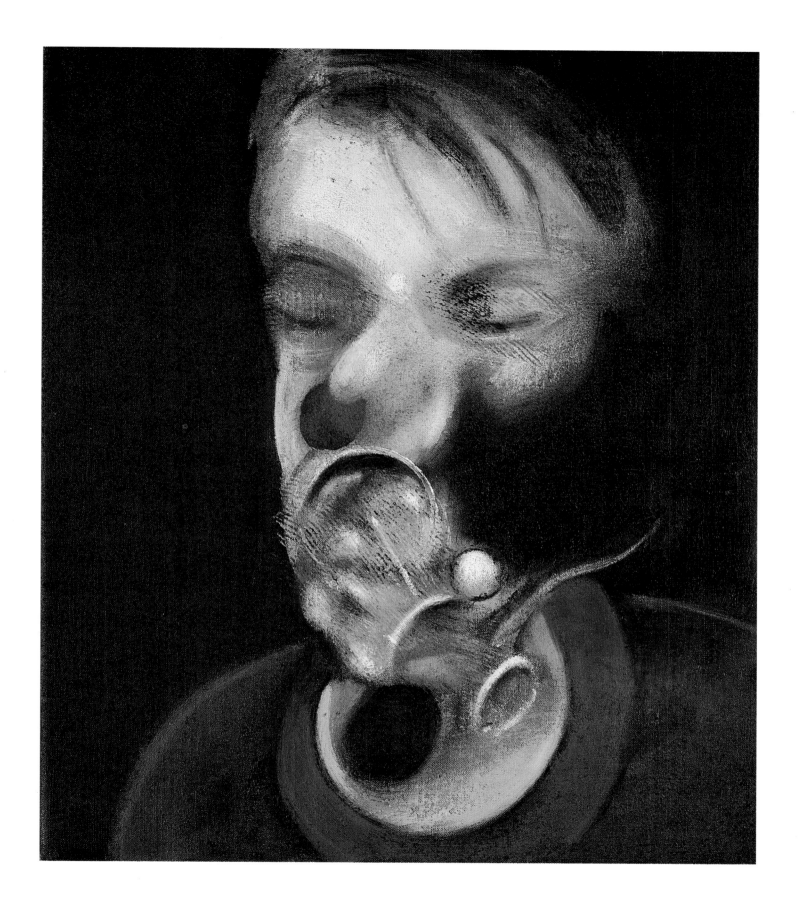

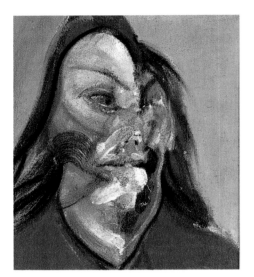  

Three Studies for Portraits:
Isabel Rawsthorne, Lucian Freud
and J. H.
1966
Oil on canvas
35.5 x 30.5 cm (each)
(opposite: detail)

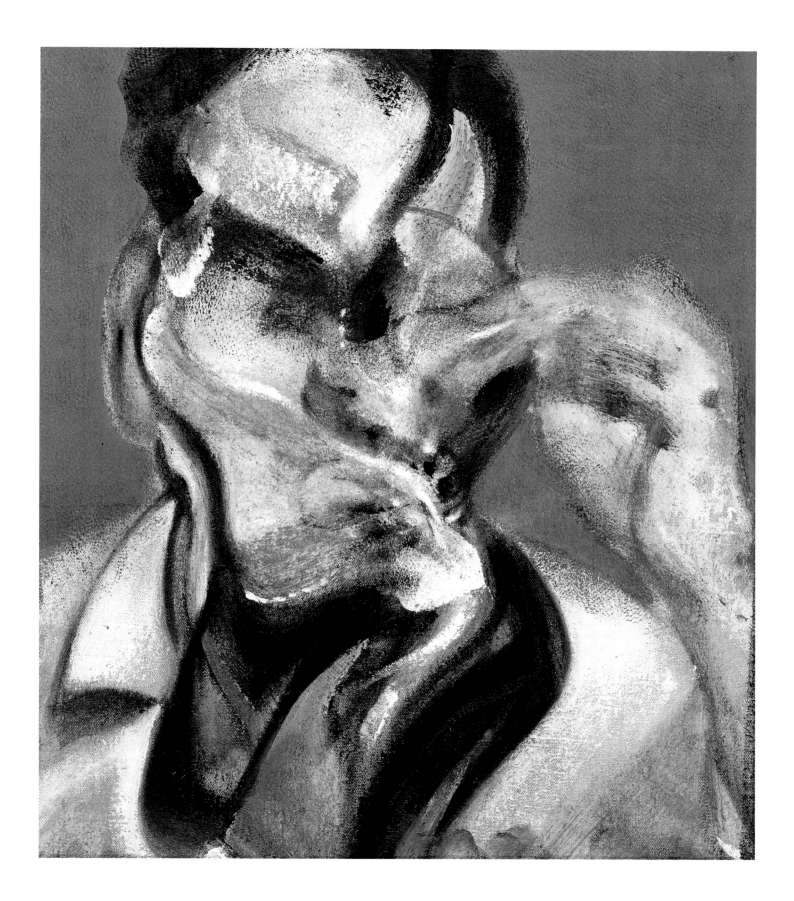

Three Studies for
Portrait of Lucian Freud
1965
Oil on canvas
35.5 x 30.5 cm (each)

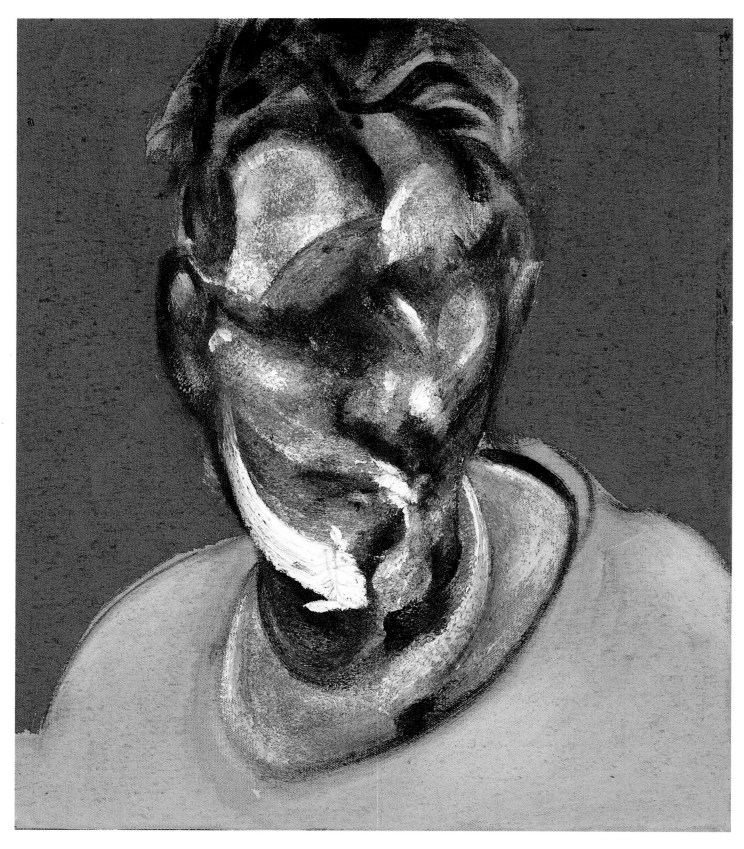

Portrait of Lucian Freud 1965

Oil on canvas 35.5 x 30.5 cm

Study for Head of Lucian Freud 1967

Oil on canvas 35.5 x 30.5 cm

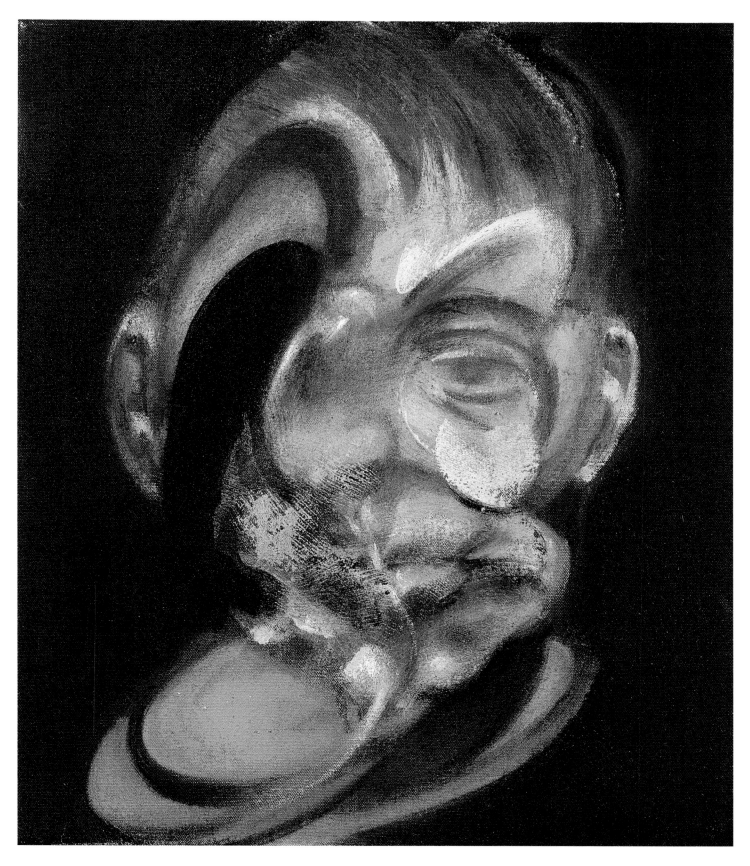

Self-Portrait 1973

Oil on canvas 35.5 x 30.5 cm

87

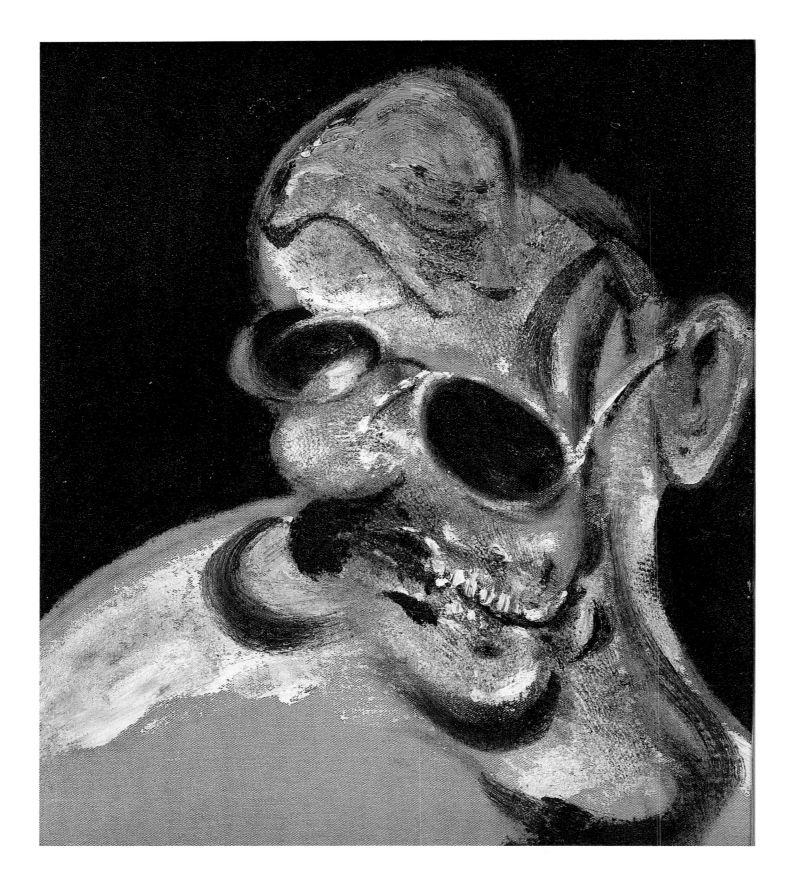

Portrait of Man with Glasses III 1963

Oil on canvas 33.7 x 28.7 cm

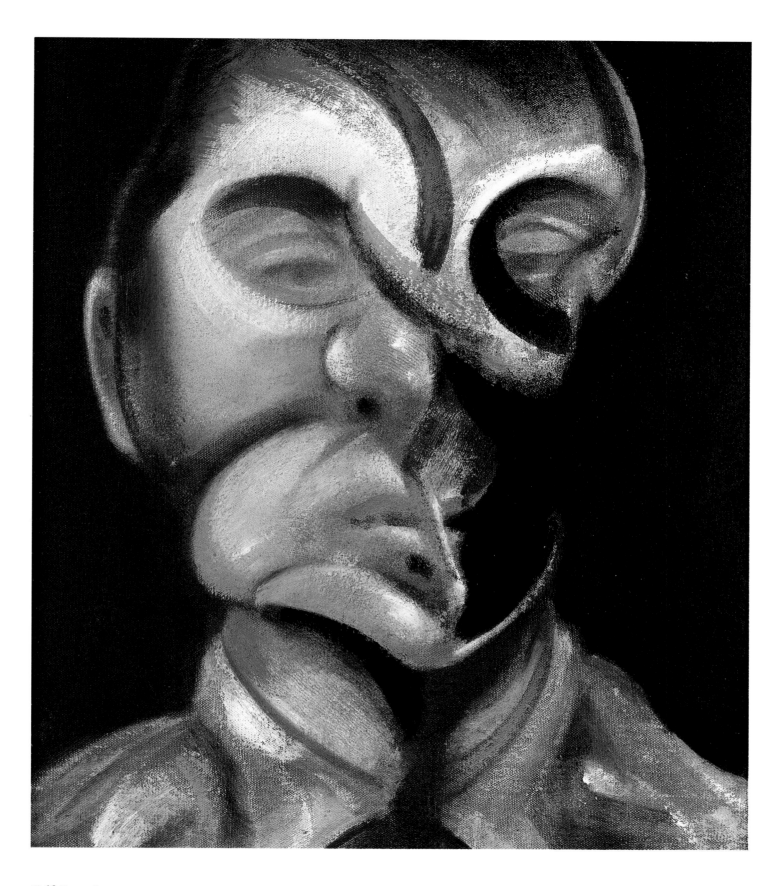

Self-Portrait 1972
Oil on canvas 35.5 x 30.5 cm

Three Studies for
Self-Portrait
1974
Oil on canvas
35.5 x 30.5 cm (each)
(opposite: detail)

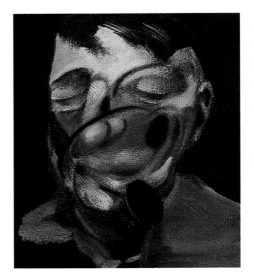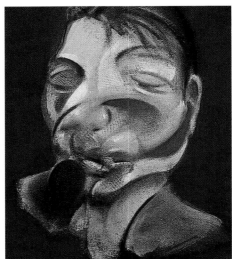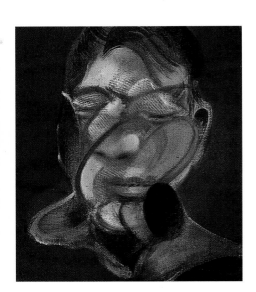

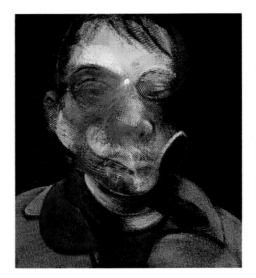 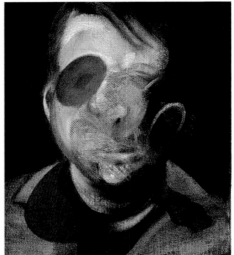 

*Three Studies for
Self-Portrait*
1976
Oil on canvas
35.5 x 30.5 cm (each)

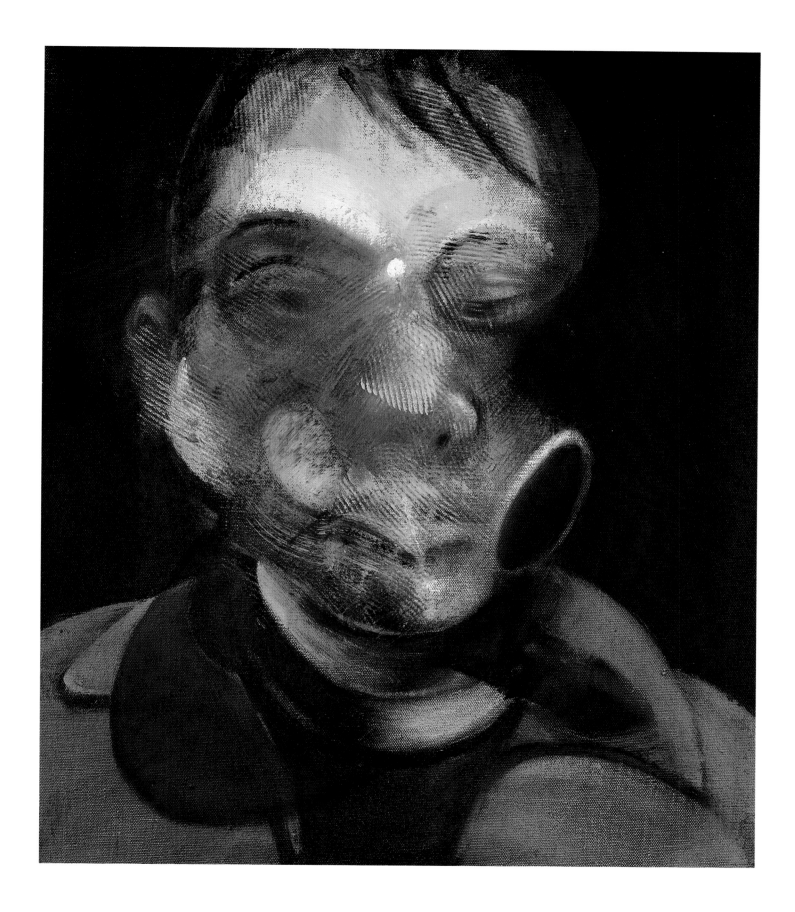

Triptych
1977
Oil on canvas
35.5 x 30.5 cm (each)

Head II and Head IV
1961
Oil on canvas
36 x 31 cm (each)

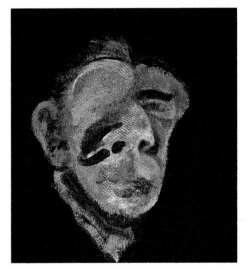

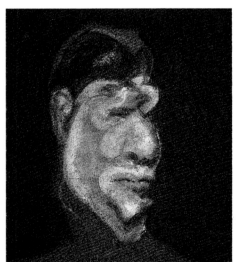

Head III 1961
Oil on canvas 35.5 x 30.5 cm

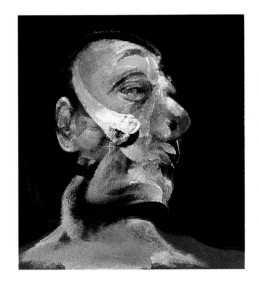  

Three Studies of Muriel Belcher
1966
Oil on canvas
35.5 x 30.5 cm (each)
(opposite: detail)

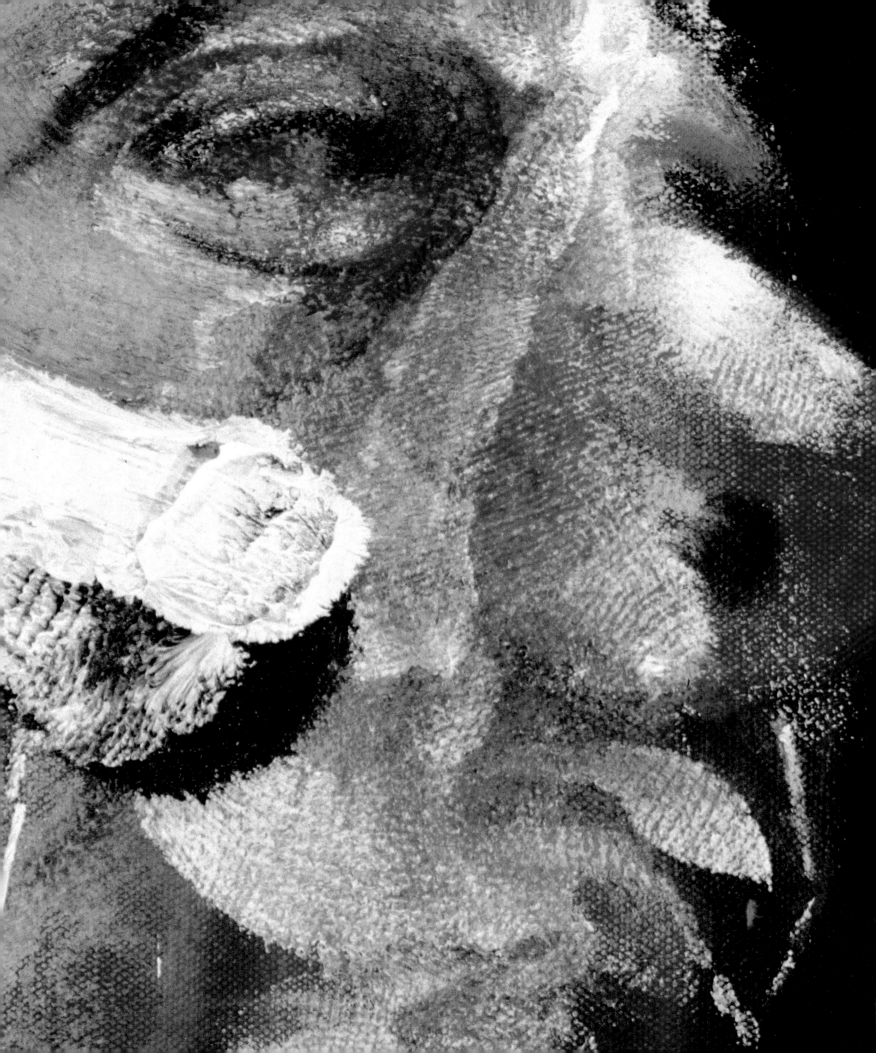

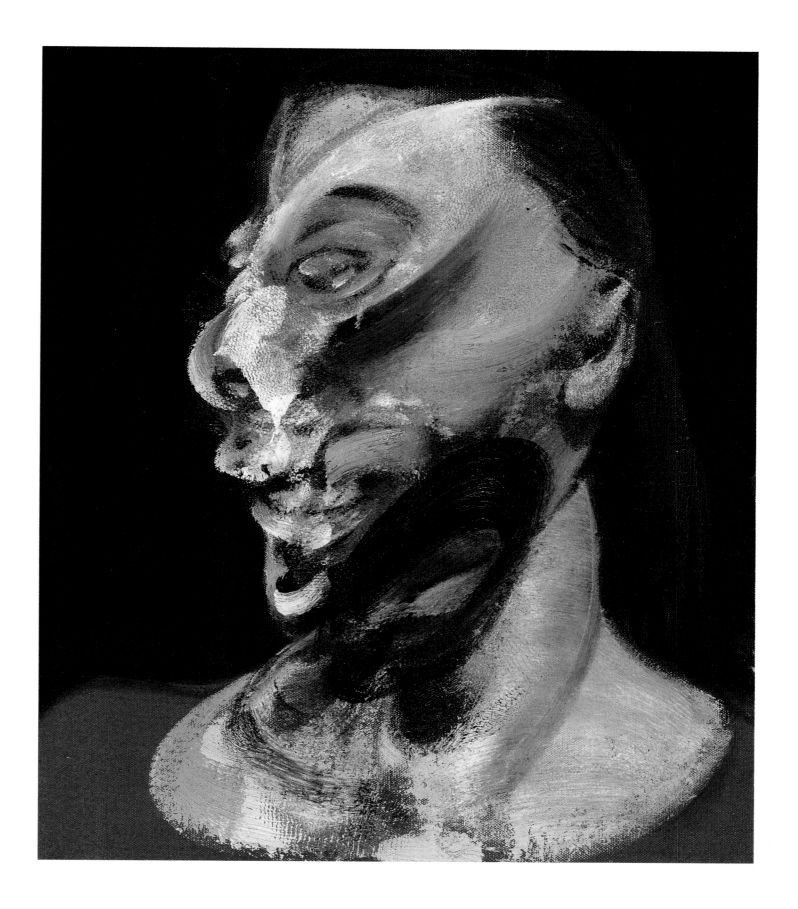

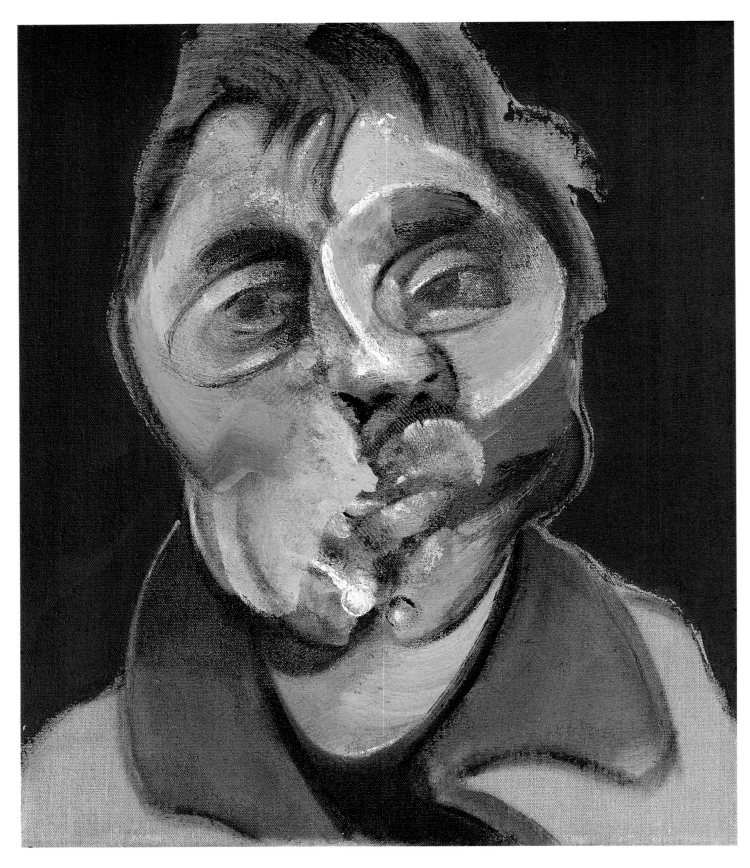

Self-Portrait 1969

Oil on canvas 35.5 x 30.5 cm

Self-Portrait 1972

Oil on canvas 35.5 x 30.5 cm

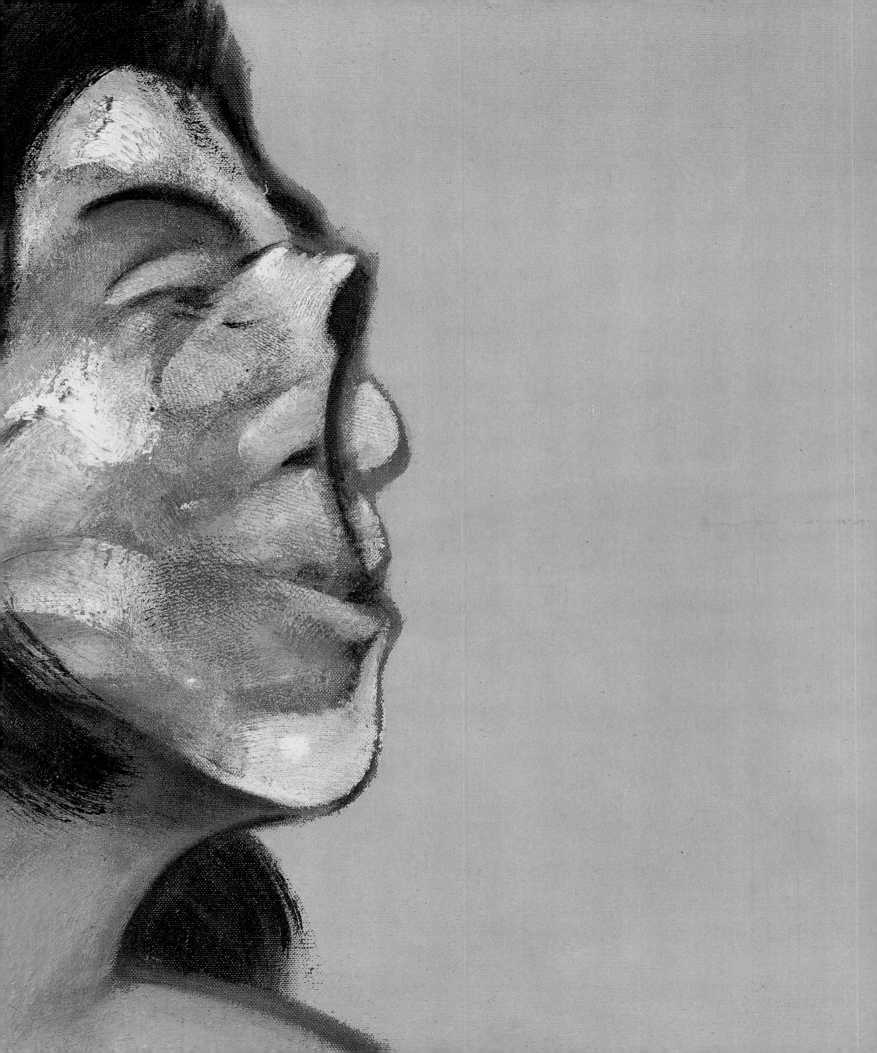

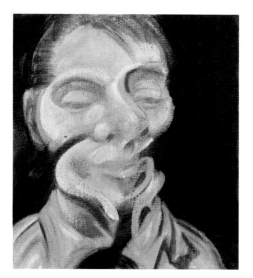

Two Studies for Self-Portrait
1972
Oil on canvas
35.5 x 30.5 cm (each)

Henrietta Moraes 1969
Oil on canvas
35.5 x 30.5 cm
(opposite)

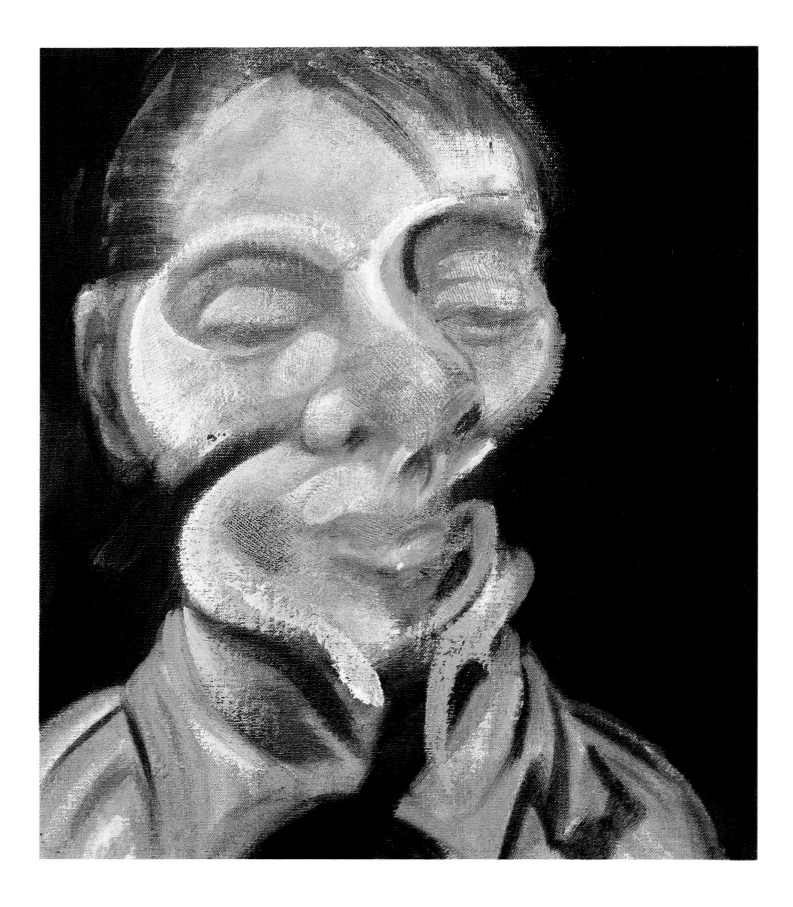

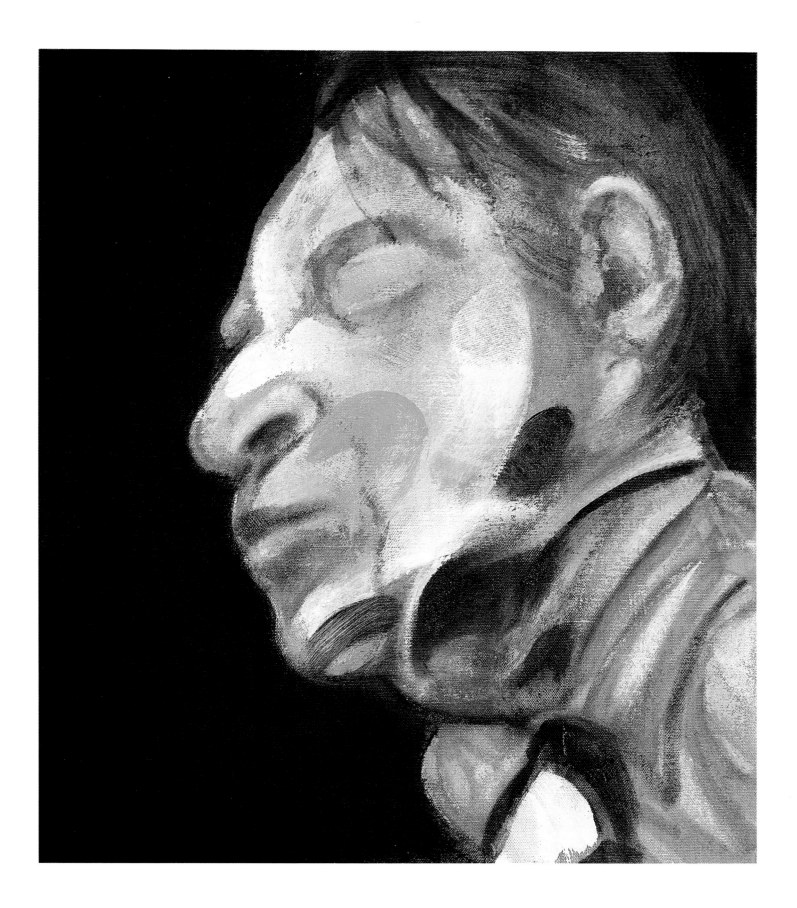

Three Studies of
Henrietta Moraes
1969
Oil on canvas
35.5 x 30.5 cm (each)
(opposite: detail)

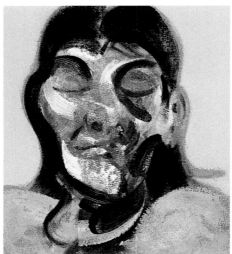

*Three Studies of
Henrietta Moraes*
1969
Oil on canvas
35.5 x 30.5 cm (each)

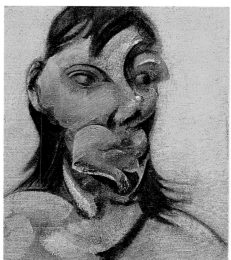

Self-Portrait 1969
Oil on canvas 35.5 x 30.5 cm
(opposite)

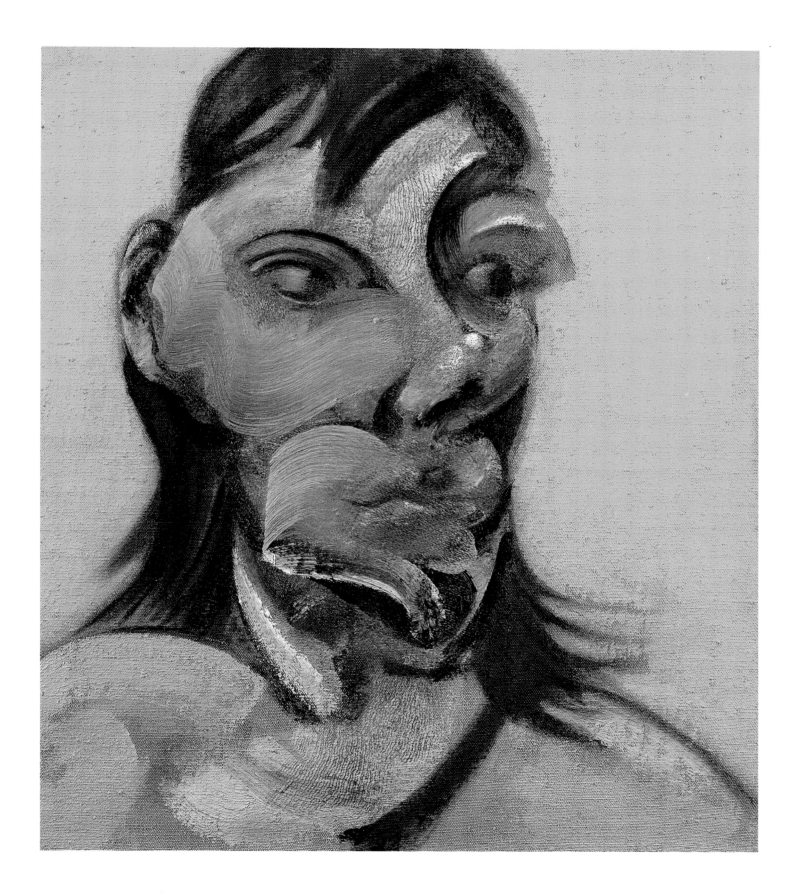

*Three Studies for Portrait
of Henrietta Moraes*
1963
Oil on canvas
35.5 x 30.5 cm (each)

Study of Henrietta Moraes Laughing 1969

Oil on canvas 35.5 x 30.5 cm

124

(opposite: detail)

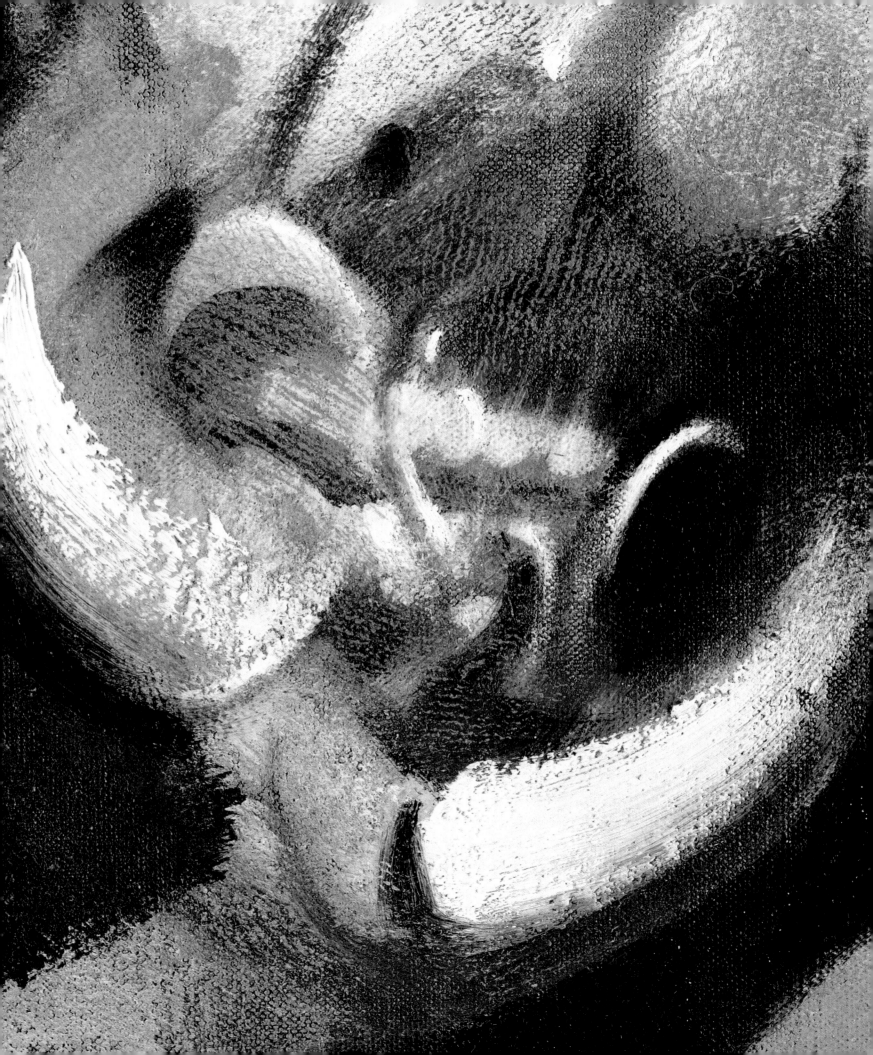

Self-Portrait 1971

126   Oil on canvas 35.5 x 30.5 cm

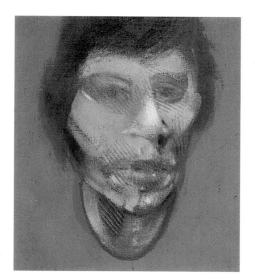 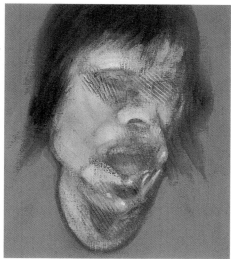 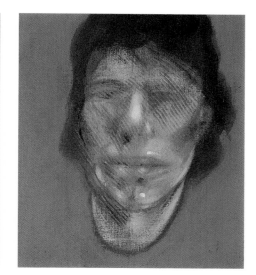

Three Studies for a Portrait
(Mick Jagger)
1982
Oil and pastel on canvas
35.5 x 30.5 cm (each)

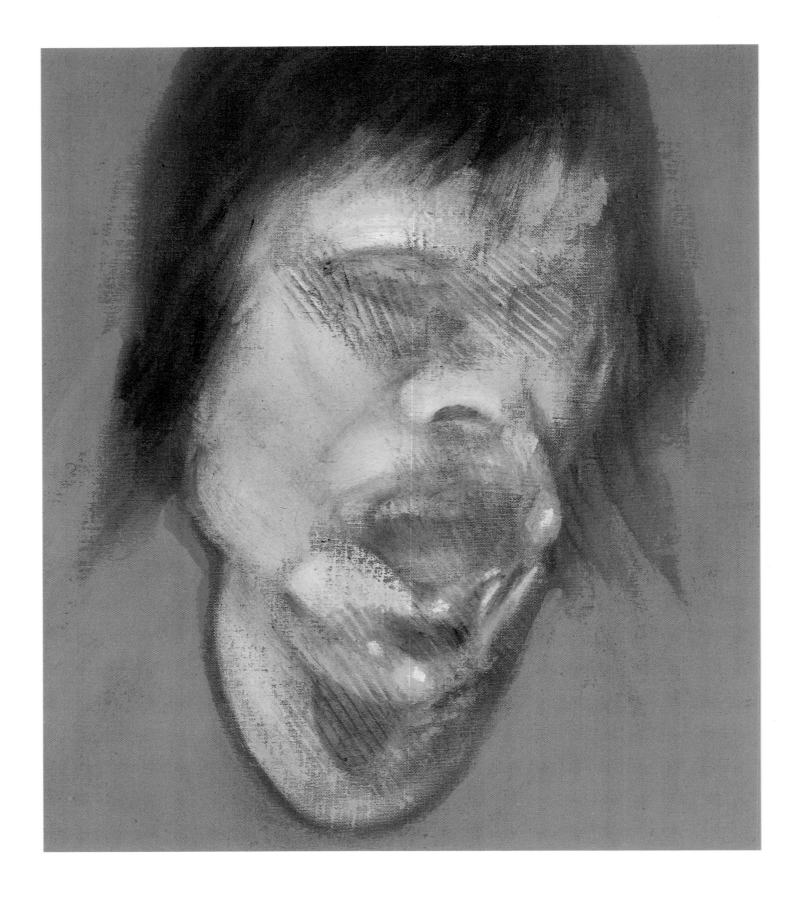

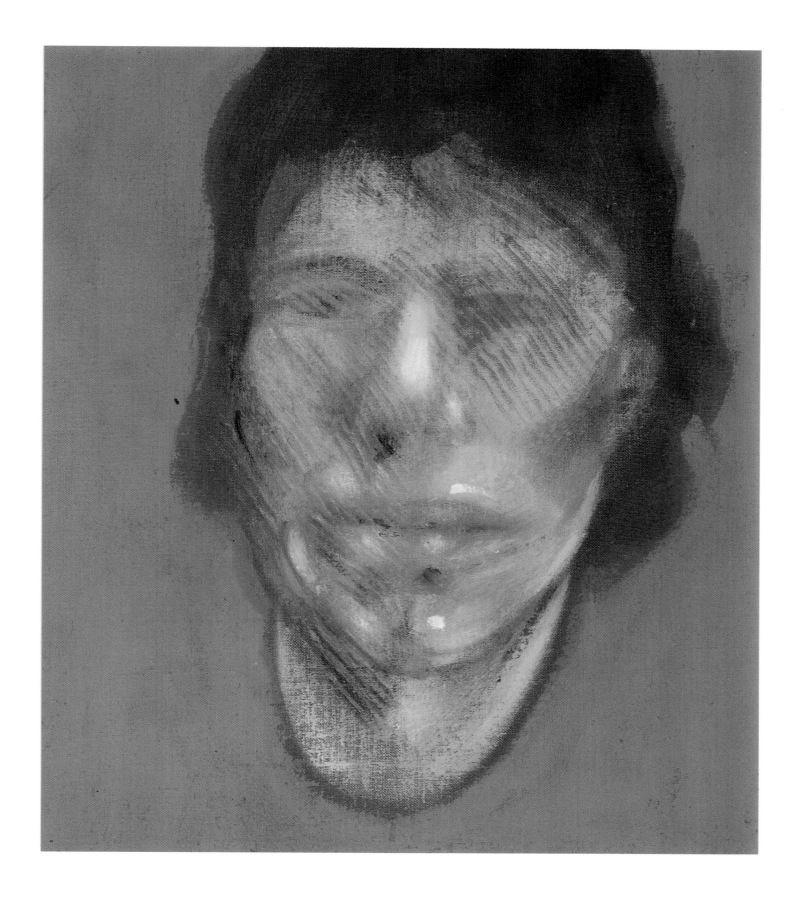

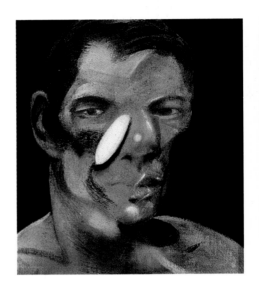

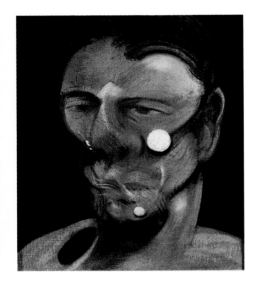

*Three Studies for
a Portrait of Peter Beard*
1975
Oil on canvas
35.5 x 30.5 cm (each)
(opposite: detail)

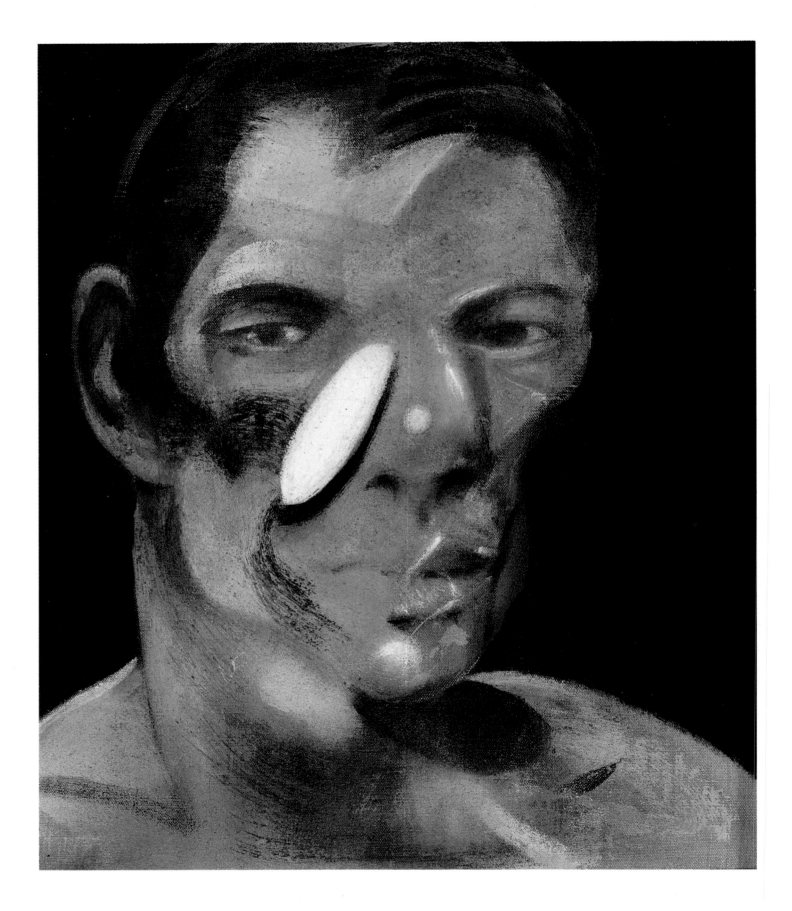

132

132

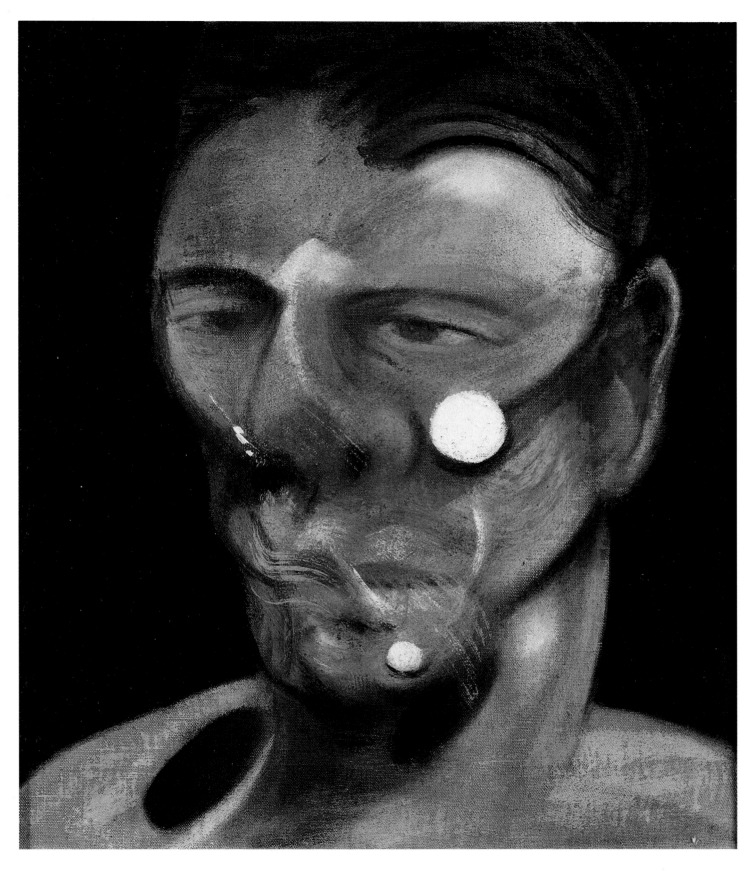

Three Studies for Self-Portrait
1980
Oil on canvas
35.5 x 30.5 cm (each)

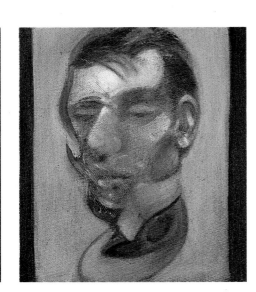

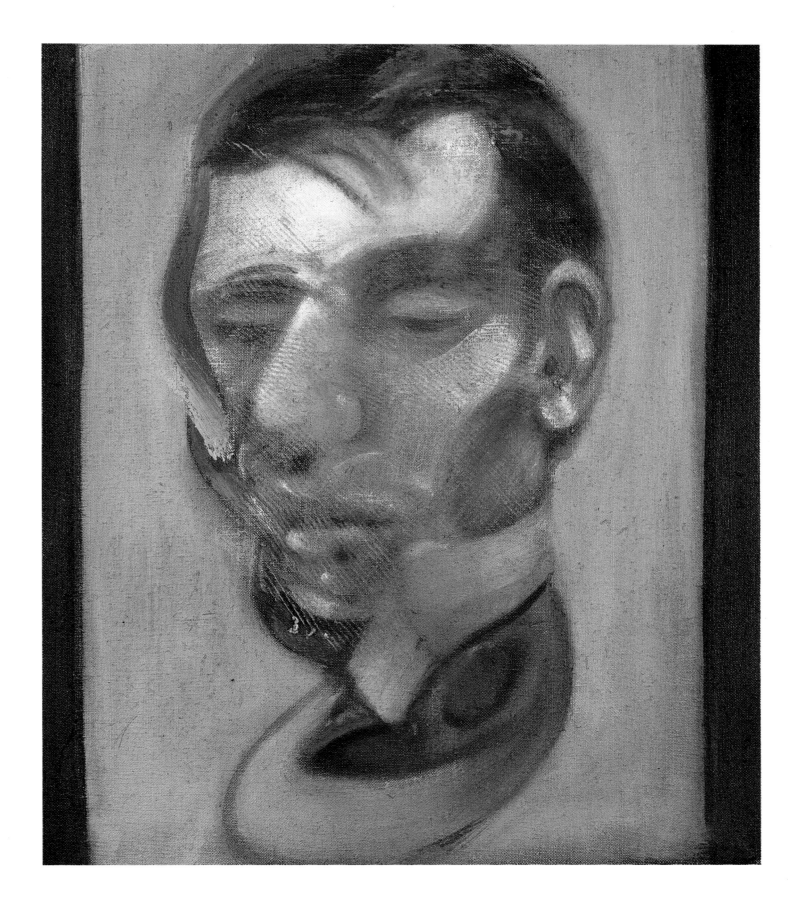

Study for a Portrait 1978

Oil on canvas 35.5 x 30.5 cm

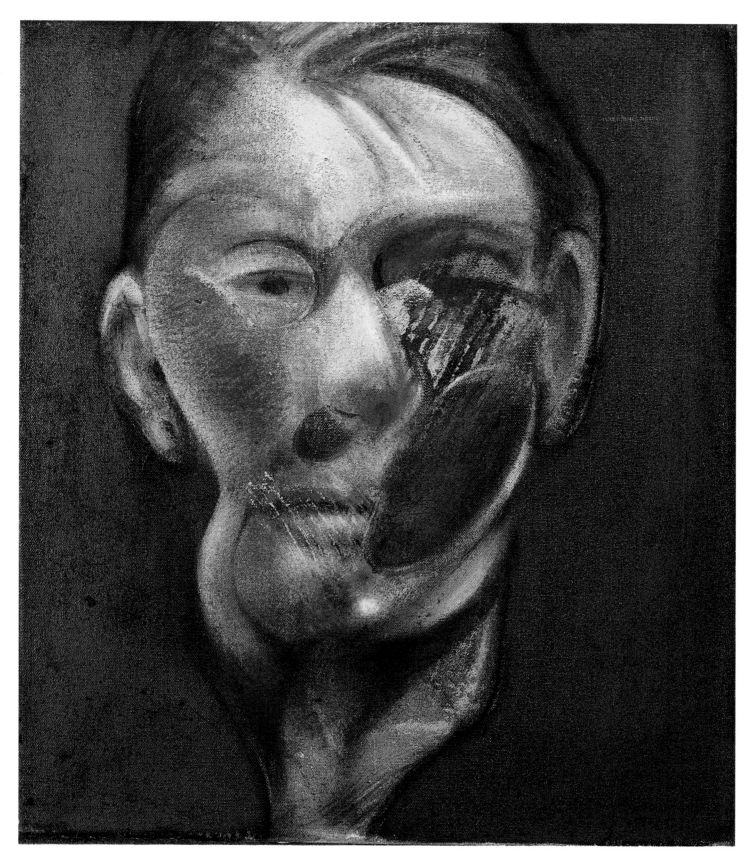

Self-Portrait 1976

Oil on canvas 35.5 x 30.5 cm

Three Studies for
Self-Portrait
1979
Oil on canvas
35.5 x 30.5 cm (each)

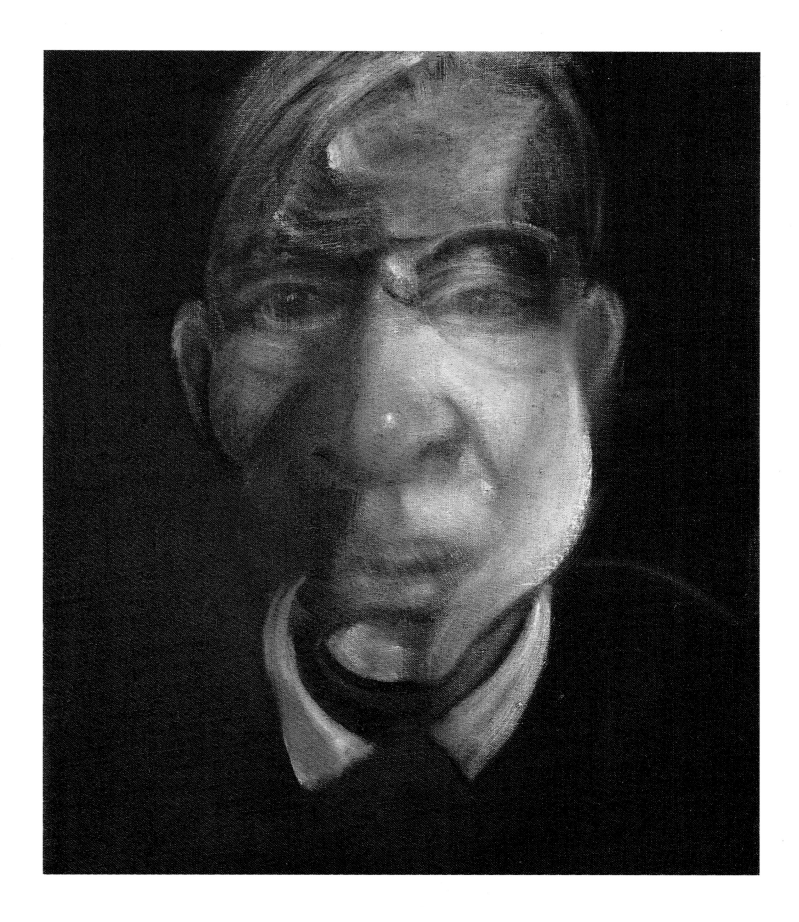

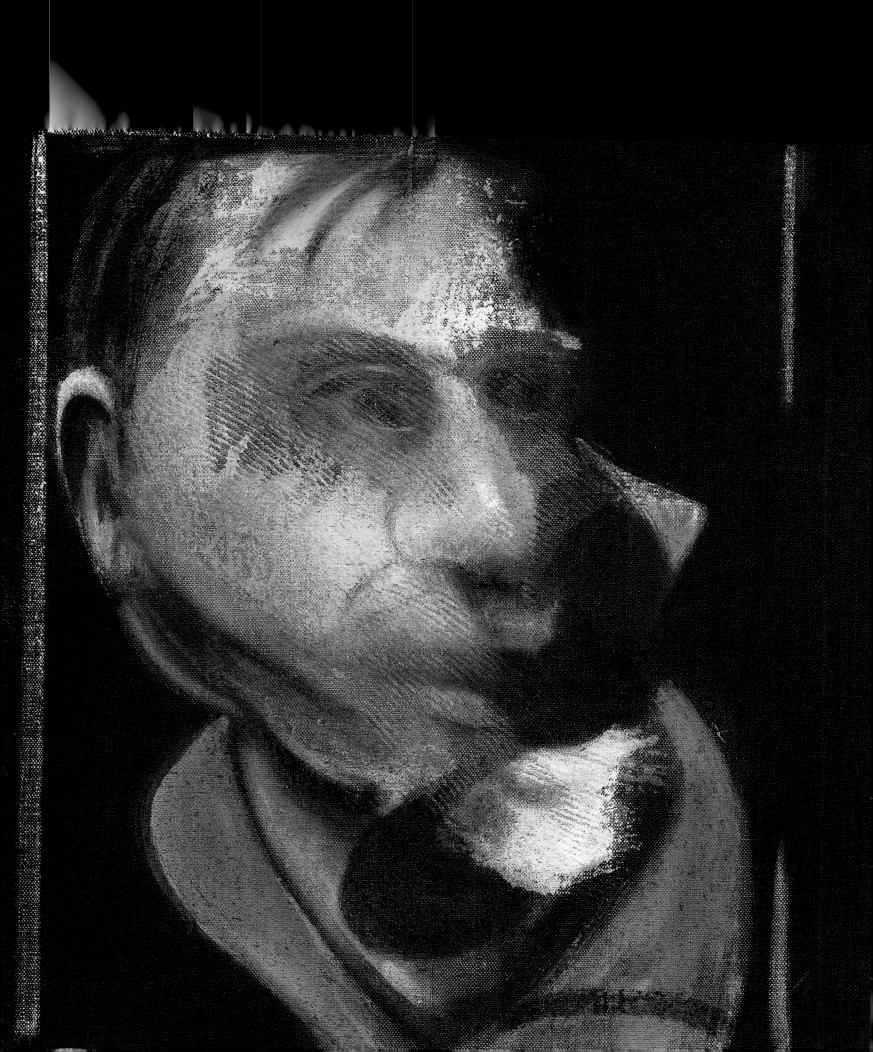

Study for Self-Portrait 1978

Oil on canvas 35.5 x 30.5 cm (opposite)

Study for Self-Portrait 1979

Oil on canvas 35.5 x 30.5 cm

145

Three Studies for a Portrait
(Peter Beard)
1980
Oil and pastel on canvas
35.5 x 30.5 cm (each)

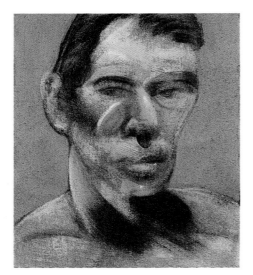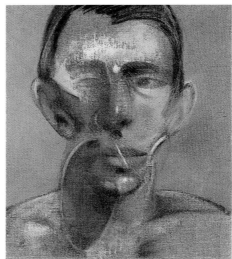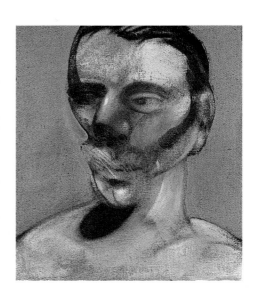

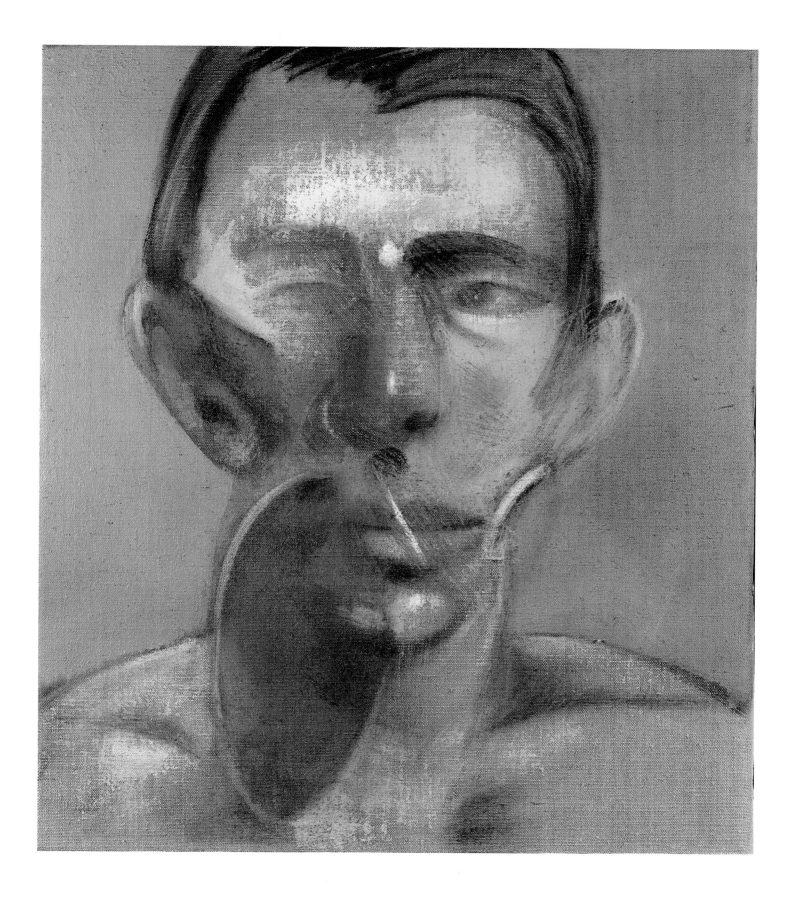

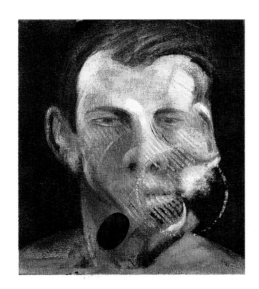 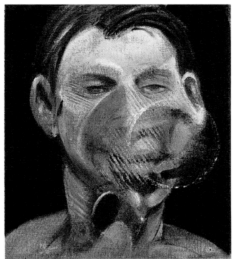 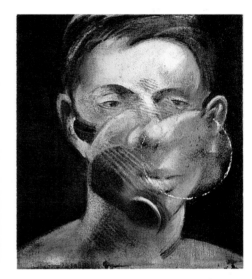

Three Studies for a Portrait
(Peter Beard)
1975
Oil on canvas
35.5 x 30.5 cm (each)

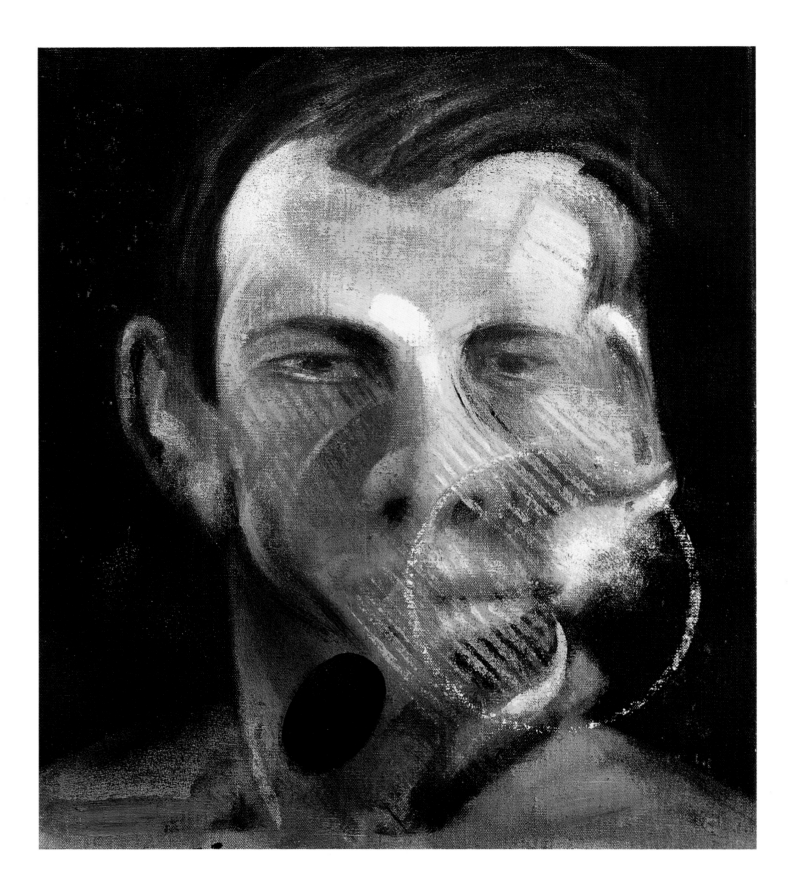

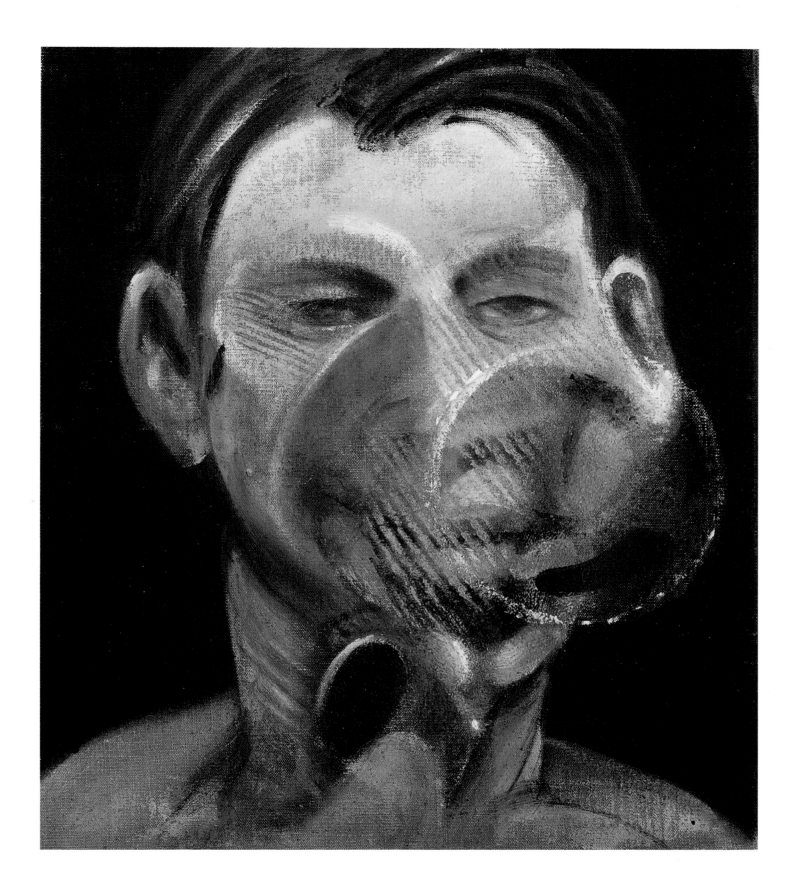

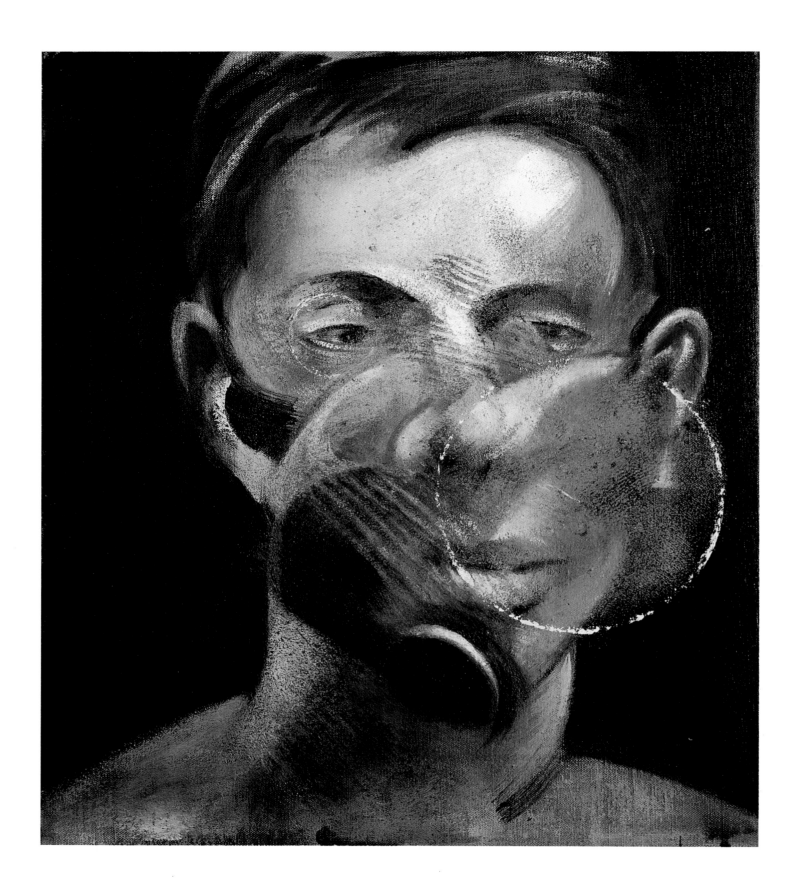

Portrait of Jacques Dupin 1990

Oil on canvas 35.5 x 30.5 cm

Study for Portrait
(Michel Leiris)
1978
Oil on canvas
35.5 x 30.5 cm

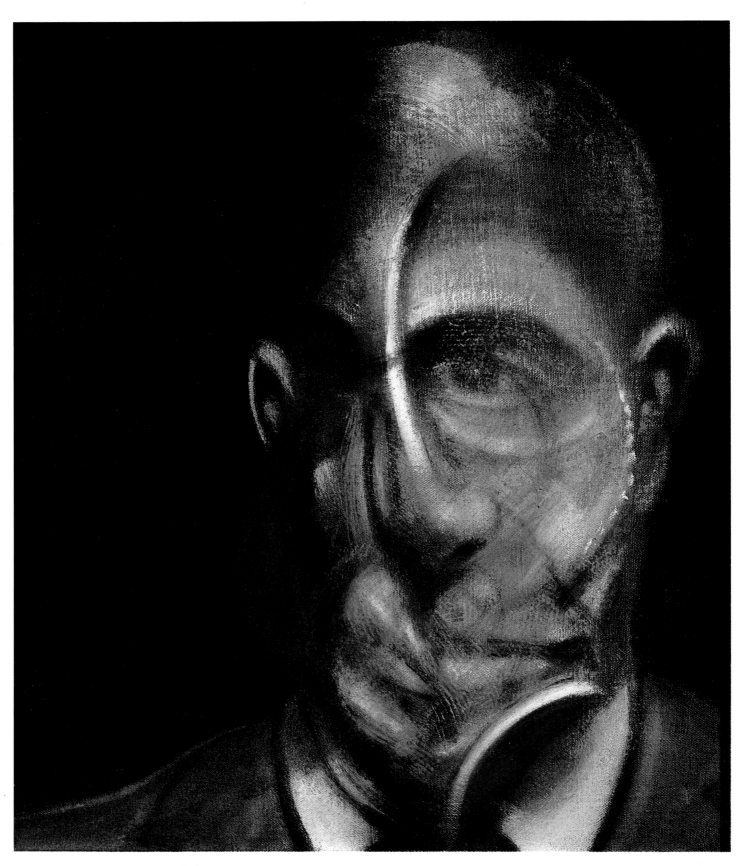

Portrait of Michel Leiris 1976

Oil on canvas 35.5 x 30.5 cm

Three Studies for Portraits
including Self-Portrait
1969
Oil on canvas
35.5 x 30.5 cm (each)
(page 160: detail)

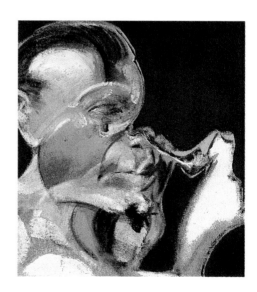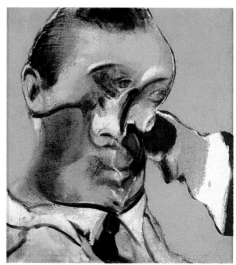

158

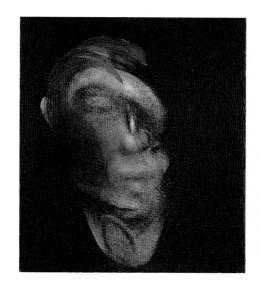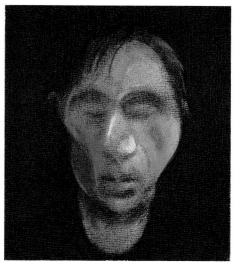

Three Studies for Self-Portrait
1983
Oil on canvas
35.5 x 30.5 cm (each)

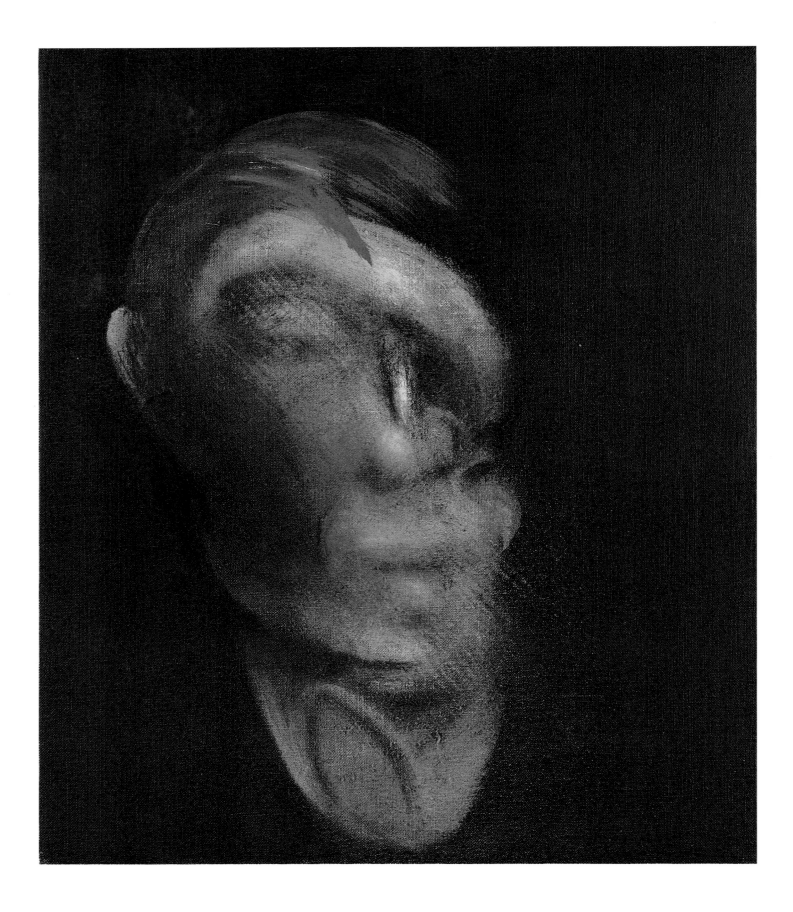

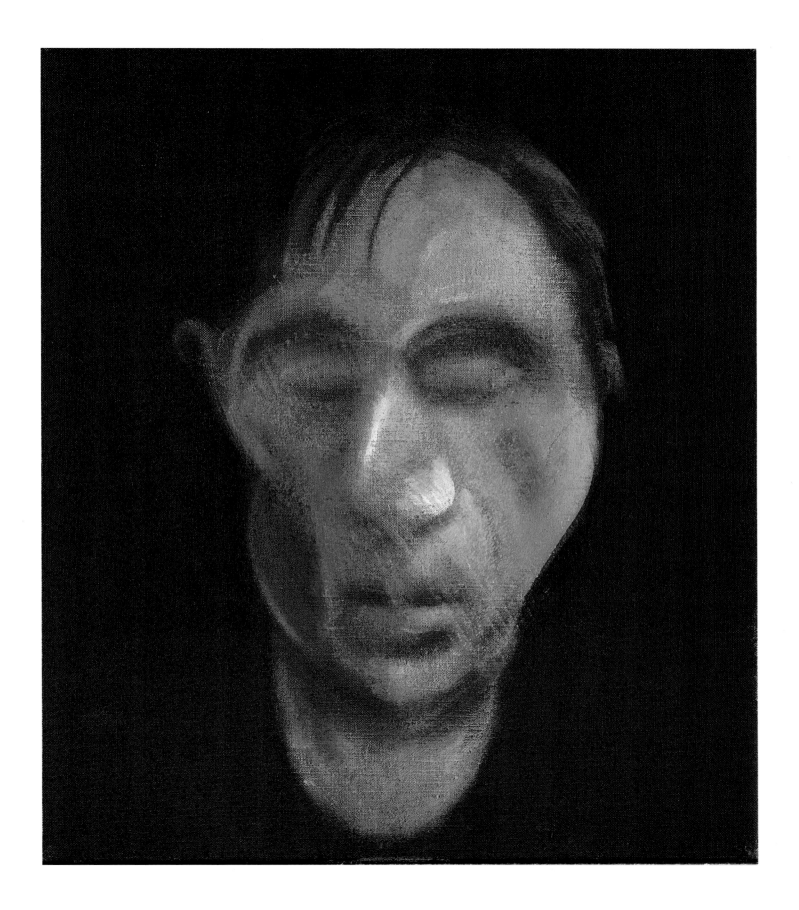

Study for Self-Portrait 1980
Oil on canvas 35.5 x 30.5 cm

Self-Portrait 1987
Oil on canvas 35.5 x 30.5 cm (opposite)

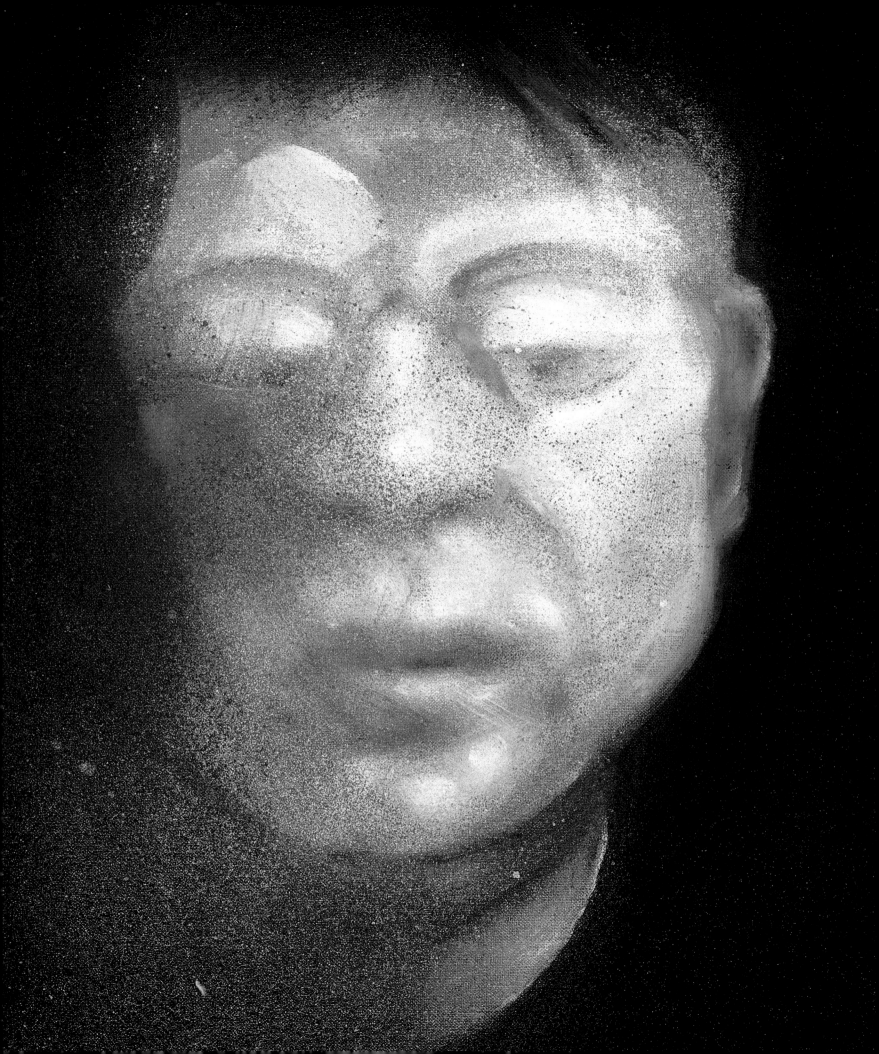

166

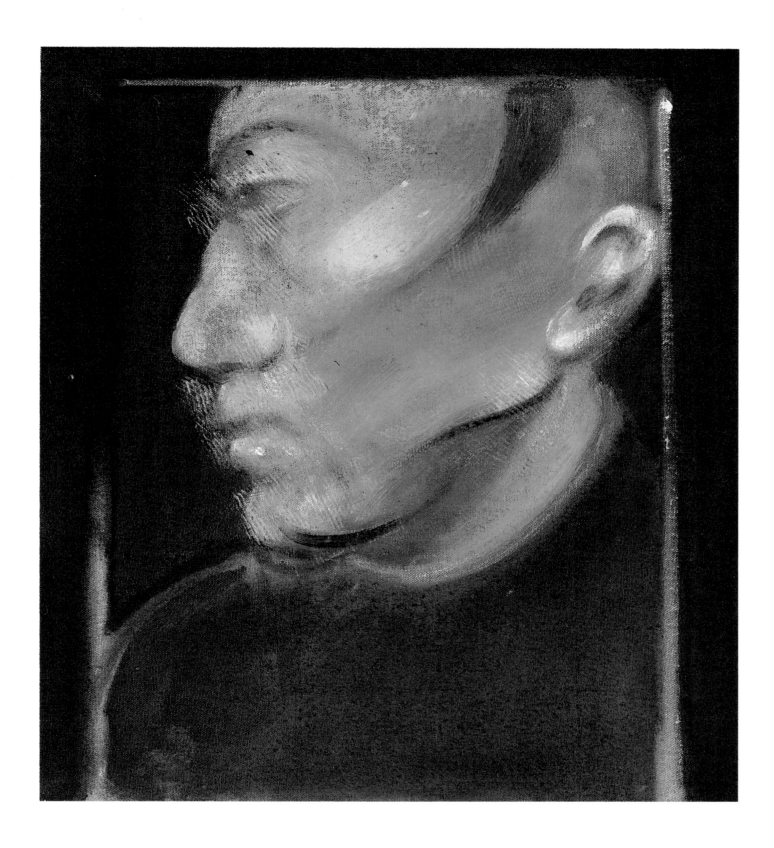

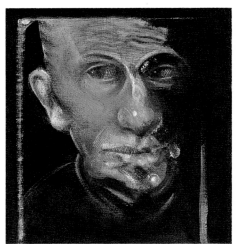
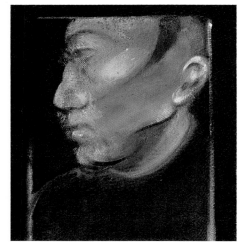

*Two Studies for Portrait of
Richard Chopping*
1978
Oil on canvas
35.5 x 30.5 cm (each)

Study for Portrait of John Edwards 1989

Oil on canvas 35.5 x 30.5 cm

Study for Portrait of John Edwards 1989

Oil on canvas 35.5 x 30.5 cm

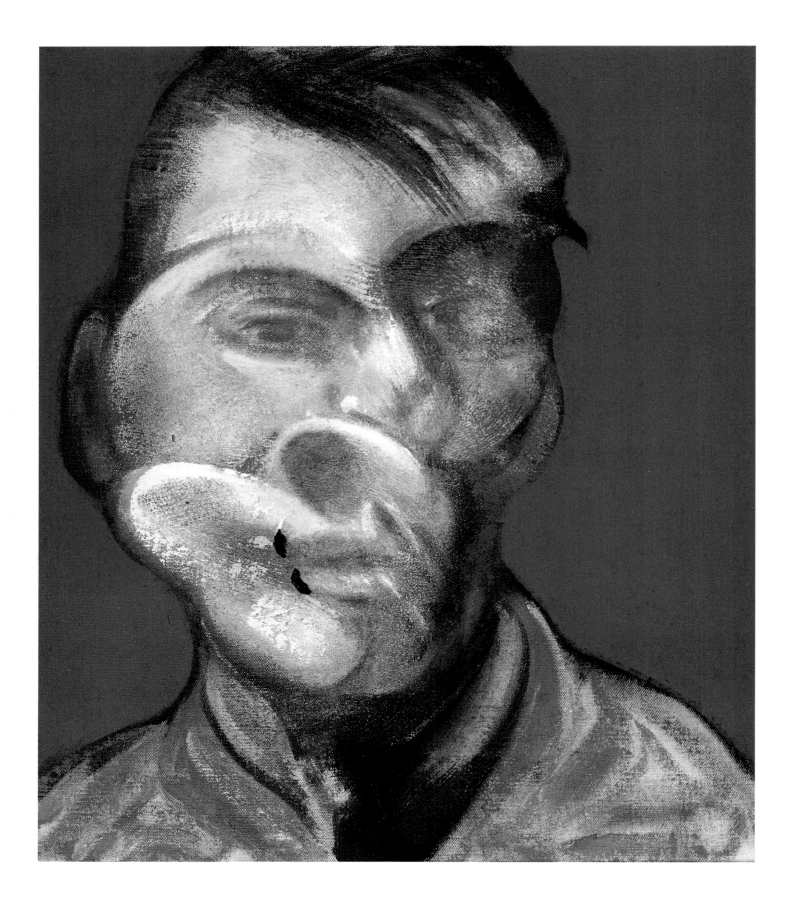

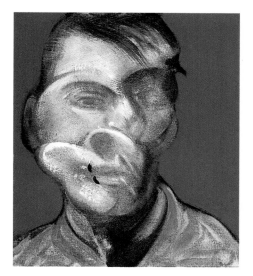 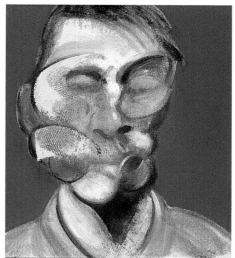 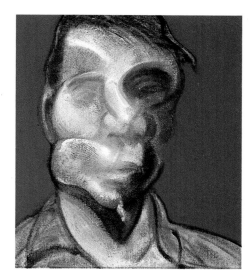

Three Studies for
Self-Portrait
1973
Oil on canvas
35.5 x 30.5 cm (each)

175

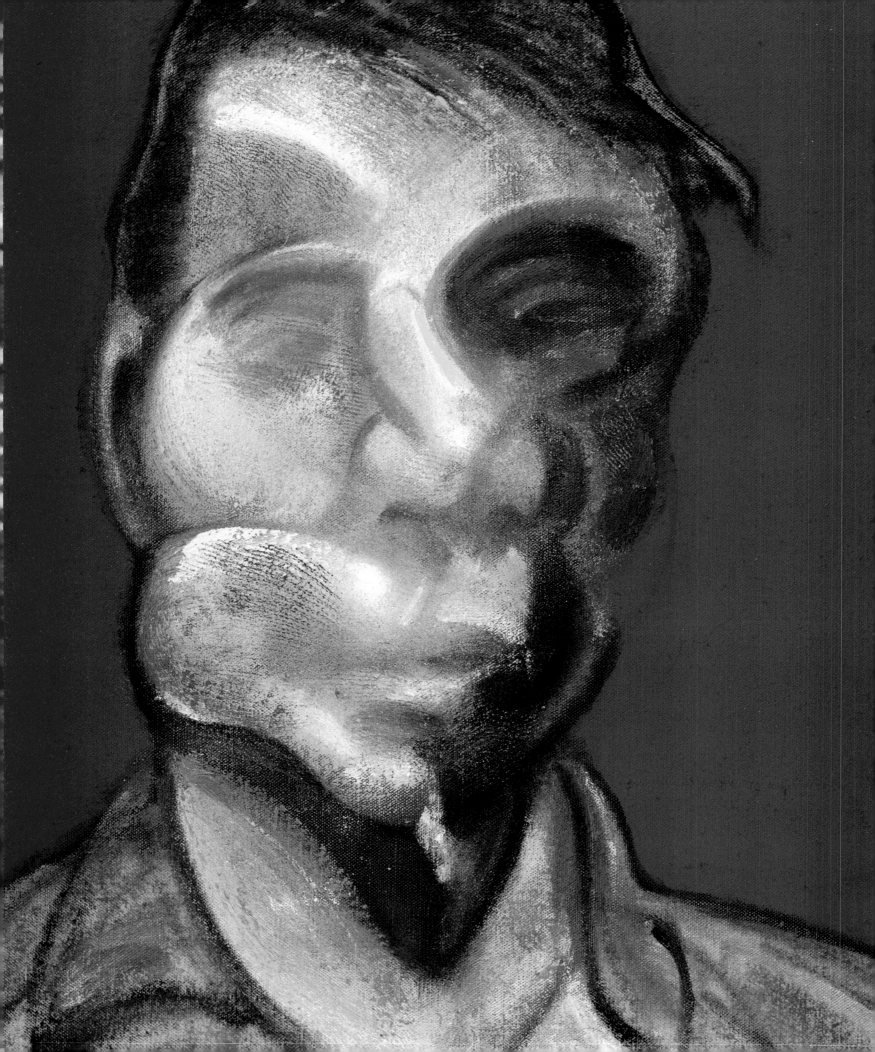

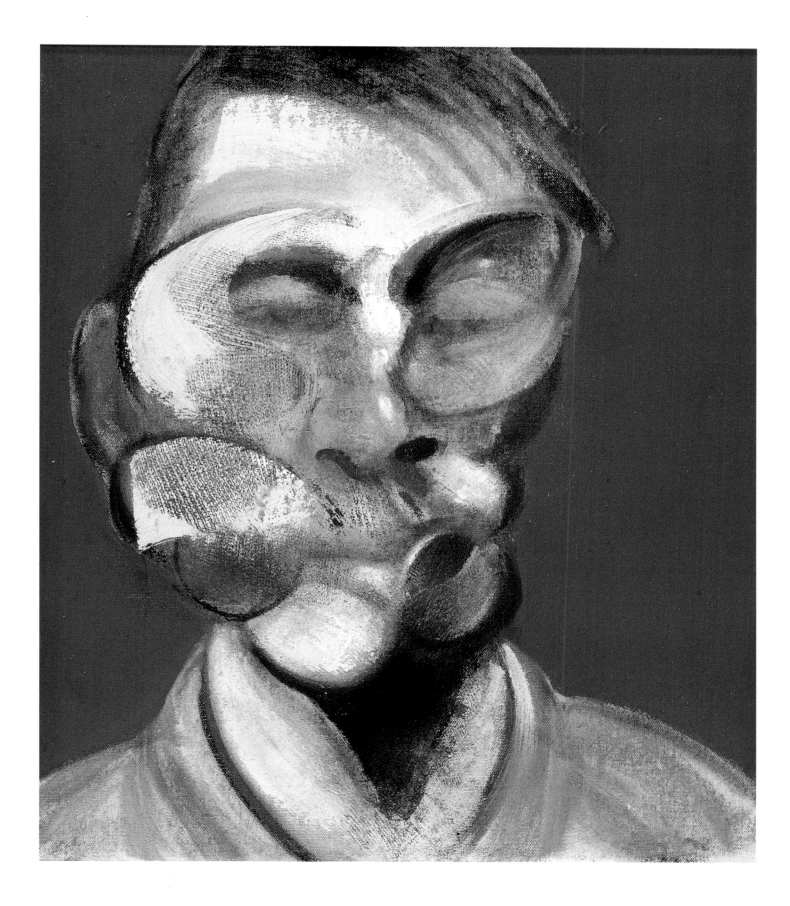

173

Study for Three Heads
1962
Oil on canvas
35.5 x 30.5 cm (each)
(opposite: detail)

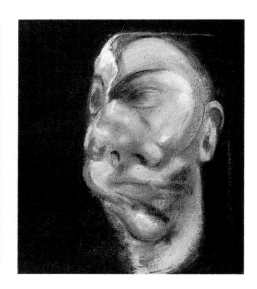

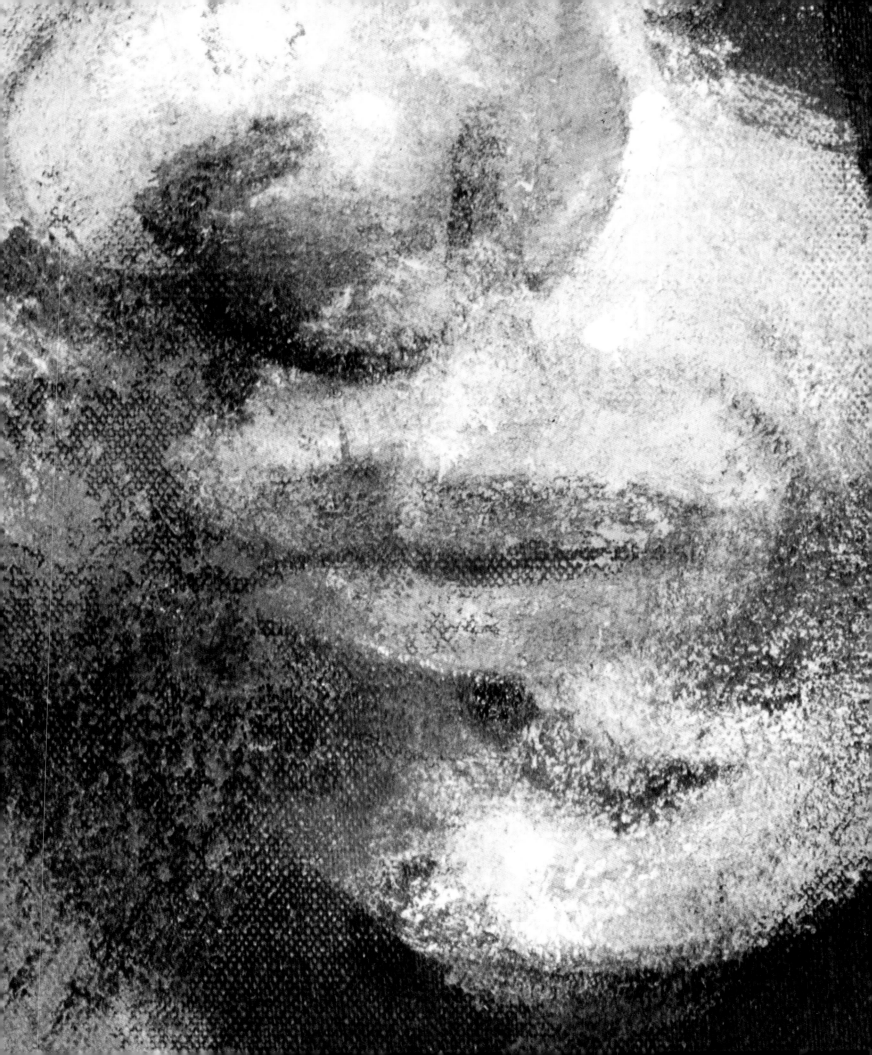

Two Studies for a Self-Portrait 1970

Oil on canvas 35.5 x 30.5 cm (each)

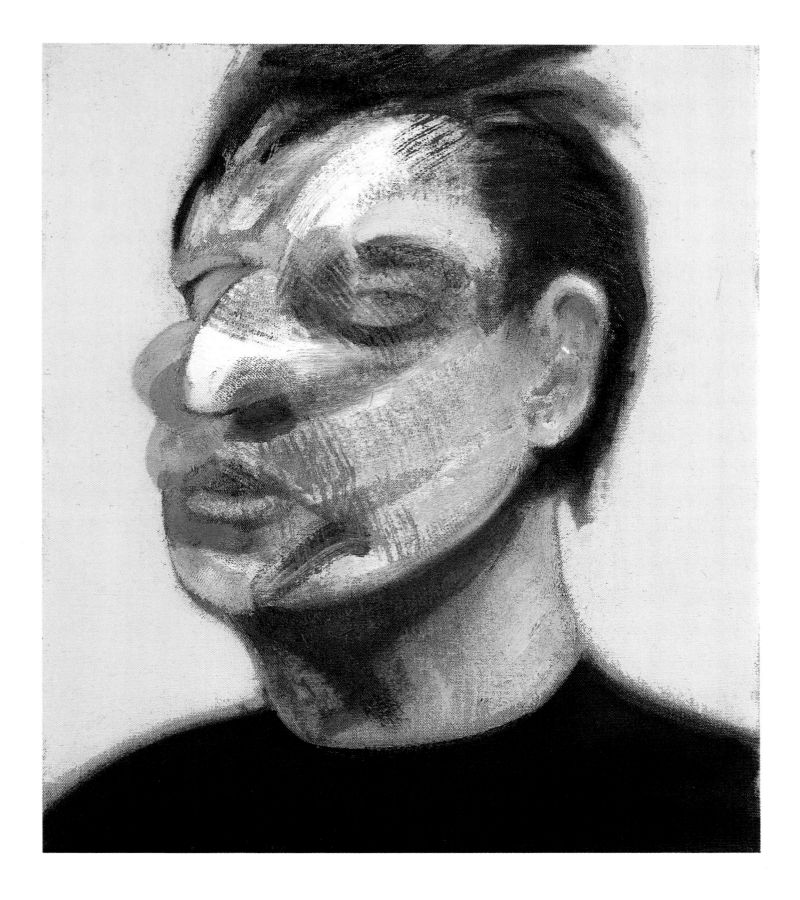

The Artist's Studio,
photographed May 1992

FRANCE BOREL

Francis Bacon: The Face Flayed

*A good portrait always seems to me to be like
a dramatized biography, or rather, like
the natural drama inherent in every man*

Baudelaire, *Salon de 1859*

The Scandalous Figure

Everything could be straightforward, clear, tending towards abstract
art, towards colours that could be described as decorative, towards
surfaces that are smooth and restful, almost flat areas of colour,
expanses over which the eye might wander, lost in thought.

Everything could be balanced, constructed like a work of
architecture with perspectives (vanishing points, receding lines), a
restrained space in the form of a room, a box. A space in which one
can easily find one's bearings, to the left, right, up and down; with
something of the familiar about it.

But suddenly the figure bursts forth. An explosion, an
intolerable outrage, a human presence, superlative, naked, uncom-
promising, in the flaunting of its anatomical delirium. Bleeding.
Not like an anatomical drawing with a cadaver beautifully presented

to meet the requirements of the medical profession or... for the teaching of fine art.

Anything but! A vibrant flesh in which existence is concentrated, denying the boundaries of life and death, of birth and decay.

Everything is there in that lump of flesh, in those knots of muscle (echoing the sweeping gesture of the artist's hand), in that irruption that is human, so terribly human.

Order is shattered into pieces, classifications are abolished, threatened, condemned, exceeded: inside-out, dermis-epidermis, container-contained. All that normally remains hidden suddenly rises to the surface, skin-deep.

The artist is seated calmly on a chair, prostrate, legs crossed, his watch reminding him of the order of time, contemporary reality, actuality. His face is bleeding, lacking the vital protection of an enveloping epidermis, as though he had just emerged from one of those car crashes whose 'strange beauty' holds such a fascination for him. A self-portrait.

The skin torn off, the face flayed. And in the midst of this apparent chaos of spurting colours, the discerning eye will recognize the person, identify the individual. With absolute certainty.

To convince oneself of this, it is enough to look at the photographs and compare them. Proof of the resemblance.

Unbearable paradox. Nothing is described, Bacon detests narration – no story-telling in painting – yet everything is said, screamed. 'I would like to paint the cry', he said. Beyond the confines of the constructed sentence (subject, verb, complement), beyond intelligence. All that cannot be expressed in the confusion of perceptions: dizziness, vomiting, spasms, drunkenness (not drunkenness in the poetic or metaphorical sense, but drunkenness resulting from the immoderate consumption of alcohol).

Dizziness of feeling, what goes on in the head and within

the body. Highly gestural physical painting. Brushes dipped in the organic.

And it is Titian who springs to mind, the beauty of his colours leading the Venetians to wonder whether his brushes had perhaps been dipped in his own blood or semen... Carnivorous painting.

Painting nourished on all that indicates life, rooted in excess, in the overblown, in what spills out from the body, even excreta. Man vomiting, man slumped on a toilet seat.

Autobiographical one-upmanship. Himself, his friends, his lovers. The one who committed suicide in the bathroom, spewing up his guts, while the painter was preparing an important retrospective in Paris.

A magnificent head, cut and then severed by Bacon, dismembered, reconstructed, demolished again. Always returning to the subject, the individual, not a still life, nor something or someone observed from the outside, while analysing, transcribing, come what may, any characteristics with academic precision or scientific interest. No, a vibrant individual, ripped apart, whom the painter experiences from the inside with which he merges, whom he penetrates (and, once again, not only in the metaphorical sense), and lashes with the brush. He even uses his hands. As he explains, painting requires the muscles and brushes to be in complete accord.

Canvases with marks executed savagely, bodily, using broad, thick strokes of the brush, going beyond the beautiful and the ugly, beyond good and evil. In naked truth. 'Painting is my truth', Bacon declared.

Blurred faces, nausea, migraines, misplaced eye, distorted mouth, mucous membranes turned inside out like a glove, tunic of Nessus.

Cosmic hangover, everything in turmoil, with an astounding energy. No sadness. Taken from life, alive, in motion, like the whirlpool created by water being sucked down the plug hole. After the climax, exhaustion. One little death preceding the other.

But, in his driving dissatisfaction, the artist always starts all over again. With his friends, both male and female, his lovers. Even himself. Portraits, self-portraits. 'I think art is an obsession with life and after all, as we are human beings, our greatest obsession is with ourselves.' Irrefutable evidence!

Moment of Paroxysm

People like moths close to a flame, flitting creatures of the night who find themselves at daybreak in the Colony Room in Soho. Bacon is with them. On the other hand, he hates making them pose in his studio. To him, memory is sufficient and any old photograph will serve to jog it, not entirely indispensable but available, to hand, within sight: passport photographs, head-on, in profile, like police mugshots, no frills about them. Any exaggeration, any excess are to be found on the canvas.

It is hopeless to immobilize and to fix someone in the confined atmosphere of the studio. Fact exceeds appearances, increased presence, paroxysm; to the limit of breaking point. One more brush stroke and all would be destroyed, the material would coarsen, the magma of colours would turn to grisaille.

The artist breaks off the moment before, and probably by making it emerge from a calm, serene background he is able to bestow a full intensity on the human drama. Just as in the theatre, where the tragic moment only assumes its full value if it is followed, or preceded, by moments that are more tranquil. Theatre, theatricality and *mise-en-scène*. If everyone, everywhere, were crying out the whole time, their cries would no longer be heard.

It is perhaps for this reason that Bacon is not interested in Expressionism and refuses to be associated with it. Anyway, he has never been one for trends, movements, –isms, belonging, but a soli-

tary figure who violates and hurls his friends on to the canvas –
never anyone he doesn't know – assassinates them, reconstructs
them in order to bring them to life again in painted form.

Prometheus (he reads and re-reads Aeschylus), he plays
with fire, eats his heart out, manipulates essential matter.

It is chance he is looking for, and he repeats this continuously to anyone who forces him to talk about his work. The strug-
gle, hand-to-hand, and then, a gesture, an accident.

'I want a very ordered image but I want it to come about
by chance.'…'for instance, if you think of a portrait, you maybe at
one time have put the mouth somewhere, but you suddenly see…
that the mouth could go right across the face. And in a way you
would love to be able in a portrait to make a Sahara of the appearance – to make it so like, yet seeming to have the distances of the
Sahara.'

One is dreaming of subject matter so fearful that chance
becomes an integral part of the journey.

There is the revealing story about the painter during the
Renaissance (age of illusion) who, angry at his failure to render the
frothing lather at the mouth of a horse he was in the process of
painting, furiously hurled his sponge at its nostrils and noted that
while the lather had been born, his application and determination
had become sterile. A laboured delivery.

'But, in trying to do a portrait, my ideal would really be
just to pick up a handful of paint and throw it at the canvas and hope
that the portrait was there', Bacon confides to David Sylvester, hav-
ing started work on Sylvester's portrait. After four sittings, Sylvester
was to see himself transformed into Pope Innocent X through the
intervention of Velázquez.

The Architect of the Extreme

Bacon searches, curses, fumes, he creates and he annihilates. How many canvases have purposely been destroyed, leaving no trace whatsoever? (Much to the regret of the collector!)

Intensity is not enough. The painter is the architect of all that he assumes the right to destroy, architect of the extreme. Controlling forces in order that they might be represented. One step further and it becomes madness. A tightrope. 'Man is a rope, stretched between beast and superman, a rope over an abyss', Nietzsche wrote. Bacon reads Nietzsche.

Painting evolved in a restricted territory, a minefield. Faces in the form of chasms. Irrevocable. At this point, the question of figuration no longer even comes into play.

Sometimes, to concentrate the energies of these 'living models' still further, Bacon adds a mark – line, circle, dot – like a surgeon prior to carrying out an operation, a target, focal points that irresistibly remind me of the lines convicts sometimes have tattooed around their necks along with the words: 'Cut along the dotted line.'

Painting is a killing, in the same way as a bullfight. All those suicides, all those deaths surrounding the painter, who, at the age of thirty, was himself warned by his doctor of his brief life expectancy if he continued to drink; something he did not deprive himself of to reach the grand old age of eighty-two, despite being asthmatic!

Every time he was asked why he painted so many self-portraits, he continued to repeat that people had been dying around him like flies and that he had nobody else left to paint but himself, although he loathed the sight of his own face.

Nobody else available!? Difficult to believe. He clearly experienced an obvious pleasure in tracing his own features, even if he did not particularly like them, as well as a dissatisfaction leading him to return throughout his life to that round, moon-like, sometimes swollen face, with the aid, as with all the others, of a few photographs, to jog his memory, photographs taken by friends or shot in a photo-booth.

He focuses on the individual, attacks him, deals the mortal blow, striking right to the bone, brings the most intimate details to the surface. Stripped bare, for himself, and for others. The eye sockets hollowed, skeletons of flesh, like the transfixed of the Middle Ages. State of transition, elusive state that engenders the multiplication of attempts.

Faces in series, stereoscopic vision, different viewpoints to lengthen and fit the triptychs. Driving dissatisfaction... Always starting afresh.

Bacon traces his features four times on the same canvas, superimposing his sum totals of the self without compromise, as solemnly as a series of images on a reel of film.

Whereas Picasso, in his Cubist period, condensed different moments in a single canvas with no concern for likeness, Bacon adds up the various 'states' and returns to the same characters with a vengeance.

By means of a succession of large planes, the individual is trapped in his brutal, animal presence, which leaps in the spectator's face. And the scale of the painting – close to life-size – encourages identification and projection still further. The spectator is there, confronted by that gaping flesh which is watching him and could be his own. Indeed, does Bacon not insist on placing his canvases behind glass precisely in order to create a certain mirror effect?

While the painter does not dissect his model in an analytic, frigid manner, nor can the spectator merely observe these characters who are so abruptly thrust before him. Tête-à-tête. Face to face.

Impossible to remain solely an art lover or scholar. This art cannot be read, it is provocation and mirror. Boomerang effect. The flayed being before you could very well be you. Of course, let us be reassured, it is possible without too much effort to recognize Michel Leiris or George Dyer, Lucian Freud or Henrietta Moraes. But, as well as their identity, it is raw humanity that is balanced there. A charnel-house, a pulsating charnel-house. Did Bacon not describe himself as a 'desperate optimist'?

'There is no paradox for the unconscious', Freud explained. Nor is there for creation.

The Sublime Skin

In the man who is evoked on the canvas the underlying animal is also expressed. 'We are born and we die, and there's nothing else. We're just part of animal life.' It is not simply a coincidence that Bacon is fascinated by photographs of the animal world, and especially by the large African mammals. He looks at them continuously while he is making portraits. A muscular strength and the need for survival that drives them to kill. In the space of one swift bound, the lion grasps the antelope by the throat.

A fascination with bestial strength and with the vanquished animal, its throbbing flesh still palpitating.

A fascination too with the car accident in which he finds a peculiar beauty. Sublime horror which hypnotizes and invigorates him. A ray of sunshine, the blood, the scattered bodies, transient postures, shattered glass.

A continuing fascination with a book bought when he was very young in a specialist bookshop on the diseases of the mouth: spots, blisters, efflorescences of the mucous membranes. Organic and plant-like.

Or a fascination with slaughterhouses and butchers' shops. Animals suspended, hunks of meat, bloodstains, ranges of reds in the obsession with blood, and with quoting Aeschylus: 'the reek of human blood smiles out at me'.

In painting, the artist is master of nature; he can agglomerate, coagulate man and animal. The animal with torn limbs unites with the seated man, they belong to an identical kingdom: 'the texture of, for instance, a rhinoceros skin would help me to think about the texture of the human skin'. Beneath the epidermis, the differences are reduced still further. We are made of the same meat.

Torn away, the masks reveal savagery. Not a single portrait, not one self-portrait is content simply to describe. They become incarnate in volcanic matter, in fusion. The most enigmatic phenomenon is the way in which they are still recognizable when the faces are portrayed going against and cutting across appearances.

In this terrain the unconscious, the imaginary, animality (the terminology is of little importance) and all the intoxication of death, the shadow of life, are intertwined.

Chaos, accidents (sought, provoked) and, despite this, a tyrannical control of forms; a mastery. An ordering of delirium. The artist dominates the situation. Orchestrator of wounds, he gives body to the undefined, he gives a face to the gash. He lifts the veils, the screens of modesty.

The spinning head of Isabel Rawsthorne, Derain's former mistress, friend of Giacometti and Bataille. Sketch of Muriel Belcher, the manageress of the Colony Room, a sketch that was to become *Sphinx*. Michel Leiris, eyes and forehead furrowed with anxiety. The constructed frame of George Dyer, before, after his suicide.

The mouth, the mucous membranes, intimates, proliferate and devour the faces like those diseases represented in the photographs Bacon looks at in medical bookshops whose 'colours are so beautiful'.

'I like, you may say, the glitter and colour that comes from the mouth, and I've always hoped in a sense to be able to paint the mouth like Monet painted a sunset.' An enchantment constantly renewed: 'as for the mouth, it looks like a Turner'. Fragment of the body containing the artist's palette.

And alongside this organic expansion, sometimes a detail of clothing, a few accessories, a shirt, a blouse, a watch, a pair of spectacles; the only elements that anchor the faces to a temporal reality. They are our contemporaries. Just as Manet wished to paint his contemporaries and Baudelaire wanted to show 'just how grand and poetic we are in our cravats and our polished boots'. Actuality.

These faces are nevertheless more naked than all the bodies, they are microcosms of the body, anatomical summaries. They are muscular like the arms, the legs, knotted like the intestines.

Bacon's eye flays his models, puts them to death prior to reconstructing them with authority and tattooing them with tiny circles arranged without any apparent logic, like targets or the impact of a bullet – at the point where it is necessary to aim to kill – or the mouth of the barrel of a gun or any other sign linked to murder.

Not a killing that could be recounted like a sensational detective story but a sacrifice, an immolation. A cruel biographical parallel: two of Bacon's lovers died while he was preparing his most important exhibitions.

Sacred Horror and Sacrifice

The faces, the skinned bodies are all the more outrageous, their presence is all the more unbearable since, unlike anatomical drawings, they can be given no scientific, academic or pedagogic guise. They serve no purpose other than to remind man of himself and the beast that dwells within him, in the most violent fashion, showing him (he who is still alive) what one is not shown or what is only shown in civilized, 'cleaned-up' cadavers.

Man is completely skinned and totally alive; his eyes prove this, as do his attitudes.

The sacrifice, primitive ritual of mutilations whose participants are victims of torture. The figures, sacrificial victims of painting. Paroxysmal relationship between the artist and his models. Excess. Sacred, splendid horror.

Bacon, like Velázquez, in his opinion, is 'walking along the edge of the precipice'. His paintings constitute a point of no return, impossible to go any further. It is for this reason that Bacon cannot nor should have pupils.

The dismembered being is more than vulnerable, he is only viable while he breathes, sleeps, cries out or makes love; beyond that is only pain.

The portraits are portraits of solitude. Figures in isolation. The individual is alone there or absorbed in himself: series, triptychs, the idea for them coming to Bacon by way of projections on a wide screen. There is no exchange. The painter has a fear of placing several figures in one painting, for then a narrative is set up and this narrative 'speaks louder than the painting itself'.

A single canvas may contain three portraits of Isabel Rawsthorne that are multiplied cinematographically. Within the picture frame, coagulations of violence occur in her different faces.

Any portrait, any self-portrait awakens the enigma of the double. Within the person represented an alchemic labyrinth of identifications, appropriations, thefts and violations is woven; penetration of an intimacy. Searching for oneself in one's image, searching for oneself in the gaze of another. 'Each of my paintings is a self-portrait', declared Bram Van Velde.

Bacon absorbs everything, he labels himself as a 'colour grinder'. He tries to render the reality that so impassions him in another medium. Painting is the displacement of violence. As Van Gogh confided: 'With red and green, I have tried to express the terrible human passions.'

Bacon was to declare: 'The important thing is always to

succeed in seizing what is ceaselessly changing and the problem is the same whether it is a self-portrait or the portrait of someone else.' Painting's ambition.

A Bacon portrait is also a modern-day *Vanitas* in which the threat of death is displayed in the very flesh of the spectator. The seventeenth-century painter equipped himself with a whole series of trinkets, accompanied by skulls, faded flowers, candles or hour-glasses juxtaposed with earthly possessions to impart an eloquent moral lesson.

As for Bacon, he pushes life to its limit, he proclaims his gluttony for everything, his 'exhilarated despair'.

The artist does not let the paradox stop him, his art is based on oppositions. Between the smooth, inert backgrounds with their slightly acid tones and the animated figures, highly textured and in jarring colours. Between the restraint of the environment and the central cry. Between the geometry of the setting and the spattered figures. An array of chauds-froids that confers on the work its tragic proportions.

The 'cerebral pessimist' or the 'nervous optimist' violates the rules of appearance and anatomical organization. A musculature worthy of an athlete's thighs migrates towards the face, the mouth becomes anus, the eye socket, vagina.

This painting does not belong to the realm of representation but is an evocation of sensation. The sense of displacement within the body, the abolition of boundaries between the private and the public, superlative presence in excrescence.

A planetary catastrophe crystallizes in a single organism, solitary, without covering, its orifices without protection. A body with no surface, with no wrapping, a body of muscles and entrails or, sometimes, punctured by a fragment of spinal column.

A suffering body like the one in the *Crucifixions*, which Bacon asserts are 'more closely related to a self-portrait', for in these 'one tackles all sorts of very intimate feelings concerning human behaviour and the way life unfolds'. He hopes 'to be able to do figures arising out of their own flesh with their bowler hats and their umbrellas and make them figures as poignant as a Crucifixion'. His figures are nailed down on the canvas, he has even pinned a figure to a bed with a syringe (it is he who explains it in this way, rejecting any interpretations to do with drugs).

The appeal of meat is entrancing. 'I've always been very moved by pictures about slaughterhouses and meat, and to me they belong very much to the whole thing of the Crucifixion.'

Meat, not just flesh. After centuries of tradition, painting is led one step further. Before, artists tried to render the incarnate, they became more skilful, invented methods in their attempts to reproduce the skin, in all its movement, its variety, susceptible as it is to the emotions (blushing, turning pale), to particular states of health (turning green, yellow, bilious), to the effects of sadness...

The artisans, the minor masters applied formulas and the occasional rare genius (a Titian, a Velázquez, a Rubens), through some diabolic alchemy, succeeded in revealing in the pigments what was touched by life, in imprisoning the tactile qualities, in capturing light.

Single-handedly, Bacon adds an entire chapter to the history of painting and... the chapter is no sooner opened than closed, for Bacon's feelings and the way in which he finds a pictorial equivalent cannot be imparted.

The Smell of Death

Horror and exultation at 'the smell of death'. 'If you go to some of those great stores, where you just go through those great halls of death, you can see meat and fish and birds and everything else all lying dead there. And, of course, one has got to remember as a painter that there is this great beauty of the colour of meat.' And the continuous astonishment 'at not being there instead of the animal'. Structural connivance with the beast, livestock for slaughter or great wild animal.

Before Bacon, we could cite Rembrandt (whom Bacon admires) and his flayed oxen, Soutine, of course, as well as Goya's *Salmon Steaks* or Manet's *The Ham*. Or, in a different category, the numerous butchers' and fishmongers' stalls in Dutch and Flemish painting, but these recount, sometimes with relish and sensuality, but they recount nevertheless and on the surface remain essentially game, a collection of hair, feathers, or scales. A meticulousness in detail, in description, prevents them from overstepping the illusion of appearance.

As for Bacon, he always goes beyond the narrative, thrusting in our guts and faces a universal reality of sensation, of his sensations. 'Well, of course, we are meat, we are potential carcasses.'

Identification with the meat of the animal and identification with the flesh of the other, of the friends that he paints and repaints since, he insists, he is only capable of painting those close to him. Besides, the rare attempts executed in response to commissions remain rather unconvincing. A need for proximity but, at the same time, one kept at a distance. Bacon avoids the physical presence of his models in the studio, just as he cannot bear being watched while he is working.

Inhibition. The photograph allows him to drift more freely from the subject. 'They inhibit me because, if I like them, I don't want to practise before them the injury that I do to them in my work. I would rather practise the injury in private by which I think I can record the fact of them more clearly.' Loving, killing, giving birth, giving birth to a work, reviving, resuscitating.

The photograph plays its role. Not only, as Bacon likes to remind us, does it liberate painting from a certain type of representation but through the interval it establishes with regard to the fact, it relates more violently to that fact. It is a reference point and above all 'a release mechanism for ideas, a detonator'.

Photographs of all kinds. Muybridge's photographs with a particular predilection for the naked wrestlers in *The Human Figure in Motion*. Passport photographs taken in automatic booths and more photographs of animals: a charging rhinoceros or Peter Beard's reportage showing the corpses of 35,000 elephants in an African reserve.

Is it surprising then that Bacon should also be captivated by X-ray photographs and medical documentation? His fetish, the book *Positioning in Radiography*, perhaps leads his eye to regard man with X-ray vision.

A basic affinity with photography, a complicity, so that, when he day-dreams, Bacon often sees images, ideas for pictures that 'fall in like slides'.

An interest in photography, too, for all that it contains of the instantaneous. That *hic et nunc* of which works outside the bounds of narration are constituted. The brutality of fact.

Proximity to the cinema too. The appeal of documentaries. Admiration for Buñuel, particularly for *Un Chien Andalou* and *L'Age d'Or*. The passion for the screaming nanny in Eisenstein's *The Battleship Potemkin*. An image that embodies the scream, the painter's principal obsession.

'I wanted to paint the scream more than the horror', he exclaims. And the scream rips a face apart to metamorphose it into 'pools of flesh'. The portrait is propelled on to the canvas like spit on to the pavement. Or a bloodstain on the floor, at the time of a murder. Sometimes, the teeth, which he always finds so difficult to execute and with which he is never satisfied.

The Paintbrush-Voyeur

Every portrait is an attempt to trap the inaccessible. The faces become dislocated, the outlines dismembered. Under the paintbrush-voyeur, the instincts rise to the surface of the canvas just as pleasure or anger cause blood to rise to the cheeks.

Suddenly, abruptly, a mask of entrails looms above the abyss, in a vertiginous state. Explosive. Blinding. The whole body bursts forth from the head in a mass of blood, sweat, sperm and excrement. Faces, composed and decomposed, de-faced. Faces on the precipice, propelled *in medias res*. Massacres. Burning and martyrdom of Saint Bartholomew.

To paint is to turn violence into artifice. 'Art is something fabricated and the more artificial paintings are made, the more intense they become.' The images do not illustrate reality but are a concentration of that reality, what Bacon refers to as a 'shorthand of the sensations'. In his haunting anxiety to follow instinct, he exposes himself, flayed, like Marsyas.

The world, life, the gods, men have torn their skin off for him, and, through his mediation, painting permeates the most fleeting sensations, conferring upon them a duration. The conquest of a part of eternity. Marsyas and Prometheus.

The canvas becomes the setting for an immortal embrace with matter, sustained on blood. The suspended time of the extreme. Rejoicing. Couplings and combat.

All those muscular figures (a sense of volume learnt from Michelangelo) in confrontation or intertwined in nervous contortions! Figures stigmatized, stuck there in the middle of the canvas (and not only metaphorically), pilloried by painting, put on display: Bacon himself, those close to him – friends or slaughtered elephants – all those he deems to be cut from the same cloth, in a common identity of dynamic suffering. Animated victims of torture.

When asked by a journalist to describe his ideal man, Bacon replied without a moment's hesitation: 'the Nietzsche of the football team!'

The painter, ogre demiurge searching for a rendition of all that is most 'poignant' (a much favoured word), skins, skins himself, flays man and beast, never sparing himself – spectator and participant – in the symbolic sacrifices offered to art in which the boundaries of taste are transgressed.

Trance during which blood permeates the canvas, nourishes it. Rendering the pulsations.

This is the Italian Renaissance painters' defiance of the *incarnato* propelled into the context of the end of a millennium.

Apocalypse.

Art is a mortal danger.

Translated from the French by Ruth Taylor

CHRONOLOGY

1909

Born in Dublin on 28 October, the second of five children. Francis's father, Edward Bacon, and his mother Winifred (née Firth) are both of English nationality. The family home, Canny Court, is in County Kildare. The family lives in Ireland as Edward Bacon is a racehorse breeder and trainer.

1914

Following the declaration of war, Edward goes to work in the War Office and the family settles in Westbourne Terrace in London. Immediately after the conflict, the Bacons return to Ireland, living for a while at Abbeyleix, in a house called Farmleigh that had belonged to Francis's maternal grandmother. The family move frequently, living alternately in Ireland and in England. Francis Bacon suffers from asthma and rarely goes to school, being taught by private tutors and attending Dean Close School in Cheltenham for a year.

1925–26

Following a series of violent disagreements with his father, Bacon leaves for London. Survives by doing various jobs and on the modest sums his mother sends him.

1927–28

With an older friend, he travels to Berlin, a city at that time permeated by an atmosphere of great freedom and intense creativity. Two months later, he goes to Paris, spending more than a year there and earning his living by doing odd jobs and a few commissions for interior decoration. The Picasso exhibition held at the Galerie Paul Rosenberg determines his decision to become a painter. He begins to draw and paint. Spends three months living with a family near Chantilly and while there is fascinated by the manner in which Poussin succeeded in rendering the human cry in his painting *The Massacre of the Innocents*.

1928–29

On returning to London, he takes a studio in Queensberry Mews West, South Kensington, where he exhibits rugs, pieces of furniture and watercolours. Lives in relative poverty. Meets the Australian artist Roy de Maistre and, self-taught, begins to paint in oils.

1929–30

Together with de Maistre, mounts a small exhibition of oil paintings, watercolours and furniture in his studio. *The Studio* devotes a double-page article to his work, entitled 'The 1930 Look in British Decoration'.

1931

Moves to Fulham Road, gradually giving up interior decoration commissions to devote himself to painting. Works in various office jobs or as a telephonist, cook or waiter.

1933

Takes part in two collective shows at the Mayor Gallery. A reproduction of his *Crucifixion* (1933) is published in Herbert Read's celebrated work *Art Now*. One of the three *Crucifixions* painted in this same year is bought by the well-known collector Sir Michael Sadler. Moves once again, this time to a studio in Royal Hospital Road, Chelsea.

1934

First one-man show held in the basement of Sunderland House in Curzon Street, belonging to a friend and which he was to call the 'Transition Gallery'. Disheartened by his lack of success, he paints less and less, devoting his time to gambling.

1936

His work is rejected by the International Surrealist Exhibition, at the New Burlington Galleries in London, being considered insufficiently Surrealist. Rents a house in Glebe Place, Chelsea.

1937

Takes part in the group show 'Young English Painters', organized by his friend Eric Hall at Agnew's in London, exhibiting three paintings, including *Figures in a Garden*. Other artists participating in the show include Roy de Maistre, Ivon Hitchens, John Piper, Ceri Richards, Victor Pasmore and Graham Sutherland, all of whom were friends of Bacon.

1941–44

Lives for a while in the country at Petersfield, Hampshire. Returns to London and rents John Everett Millais's former studio in Cromwell Place, South Kensington. Declared unfit for service on account of his asthma, he is assigned to the Civil Defence Corps (ARP). Destroys most of his earlier work, with the exception of a dozen oil paintings.

1944

Starts to paint again, notably *Three Studies for Figures at the Base of a Crucifixion*, a work strongly influenced by Picasso. This triptych is exhibited at the Lefevre Gallery in London in April 1945, being subsequently acquired by the Tate Gallery in London in 1953.

1945–46

Exhibits in collective shows in London, as well as at an international exhibition of modern art held at UNESCO in Paris. *Painting,* of 1946, is bought by Erica Brausen, who was subsequently to become his agent and dealer. This canvas was later acquired by Alfred Barr in 1948 for the Museum of Modern Art in New York.

1946–50

Frequent periods spent in Monte Carlo in the company of Graham Sutherland. One-man shows at the Hanover Gallery, London. Begins work on the series of *Heads*, of which *Head VI* is considered as the first of his series of *Popes*. Uses Eadweard Muybridge's photographic studies as a source of reference for his paintings of animals and human figures. In 1950, visits his mother who had settled in South Africa, spending several days in Cairo *en route*. Teaches for a period at the Royal College of Art, London.

1951–54

Moves studio several times and, in 1953, shares a flat with David Sylvester for a while. Takes part in numerous collective shows. Paints his first portrait of an identifiable person, *Lucian Freud*, as well as his first *Popes*. In 1952, travels to South Africa again. Exhibits landscapes inspired by Africa and the South of France. In October–November 1953, has his first one-man show abroad, held at Durlacher Brothers in New York. Paints *Two Figures (The Wrestlers)*, generally considered one of his most important works. In 1954, paints the series *Man in Blue*. With Lucian Freud and Ben Nicholson, represents Great Britain at the 27th Venice Biennale. He does not attend the Biennale, but visits Ostia and Rome. Owing to illness, he does not go to see Velázquez's *Portrait of Pope Innocent X*, a reproduction of which provided the inspiration for his *Popes*.

1955

First retrospective exhibition of his work held at the Institute of Contemporary Arts in London. Collective exhibition at the Hanover Gallery, where he shows portraits of William Blake. Takes part in numerous group shows in the United States. Paints the portraits of the collectors Robert and Lisa Sainsbury, who become his patrons.

1956

In the summer, makes his first trip to Tangier to visit his friend Peter Lacy. Rents the apartment where he was frequently to stay during the next three years. Paints his first *Self-Portrait*.

1957

First one-man show in Paris (Galerie Rive Droite). Exhibits his *Van Gogh* series at the Hanover Gallery.

1958

First one-man show in Italy (a retrospective held successively in Turin, Milan and Rome). Leaves the Hanover Gallery, signing a contract with Marlborough Fine Art in London. Represents Great Britain at the Carnegie Institute in Pittsburgh.

1959

Exhibits at the 5th São Paulo Bienal. Takes part in collective shows in Paris, New York and Kassel, West Germany. Paints for a while at St Ives in Cornwall, where he executes from memory a portrait of Muriel Belcher, owner of the Colony Club, his favourite stopping-off place in Soho.

1960

First exhibition at Marlborough Fine Art in London. Numerous other shows throughout Europe and the United States.

1961

Settles in Reece Mews, South Kensington, above a garage. This was to be his last studio, which he would occupy until his death.

1962

Paints his first large triptych, *Three Studies for a Crucifixion*, acquired by the Solomon R. Guggenheim Museum in New York. Major retrospective of his work at the Tate Gallery in London subsequently shown with a few alterations in Mannheim, Turin, Zurich and Amsterdam. Death of Peter Lacy. Friendship with Alberto Giacometti.

1963–64

Retrospective at the Solomon R. Guggenheim Museum in New York, subsequently shown in Chicago and Houston. Friendship with George Dyer, of whom he was to paint numerous portraits. First portrait of Isabel Rawsthorne. The Musée National d'Art Moderne in Paris acquires *Three Figures in a Room*. The Moderna Museet in Stockholm buys *Double Portrait of Lucian Freud and Frank Auerbach*.

1965

Retrospective at the Kunstverein in Hamburg, subsequently shown in Stockholm and Dublin. Paints his great *Crucifixion*, a triptych acquired by the Bayerische Staatsgemäldesammlungen, Munich.

1966–67

Exhibits at the Galerie Maeght in Paris and attends the opening. Winner of the Rubens Prize awarded by the city of Siegen and of the Carnegie Institute Award in Painting at the Pittsburgh World Fair, the only awards he was to accept in his lifetime.

1968

Brief stay in New York for the opening of a show of his recent paintings at the Marlborough–Gerson Gallery.

1971–72

Major retrospective at the Grand Palais in Paris, then at the Kunsthalle, Düsseldorf. Death of his companion and model George Dyer in Paris. Paints the large *Triptych 1971* in his memory.

1972–74

Badly affected by the death of George Dyer, he executes a series of three large triptychs (sometimes known as *Black Triptychs, 1972, 1973, 1974*), as well as numerous self-portraits. Meets John Edwards, who was to become his companion and model.

1975

Major exhibition entitled 'Francis Bacon: Recent Paintings 1968–1974' organized by Henry Geldzahler at the Metropolitan Museum of Art. Visits New York for the opening. Portraits of Peter Beard.

1976

First portrait of Michel Leiris.

1977

Attends the opening of his exhibition at the Galerie Claude Bernard in Paris, which meets with considerable public acclaim. Brief stay in Rome, where he visits Balthus.

1978–79

Paints the second portrait of Michel Leiris, as well as *Sphinx – Portrait of Muriel Belcher*, who had died shortly before.

1980

The Tate Gallery in London acquires his *Triptych August 1972*.

1981

Paints the *Triptych Inspired by the Oresteia of Aeschylus*.

1983

First exhibition in Japan (Tokyo, Kyoto and Nagoya).

1984

Paints a large triptych, *Three Studies for a Portrait of John Edwards*.

1985–86

Major retrospective at the Tate Gallery in London, subsequently shown in Stuttgart and Berlin. Returns to Berlin for the first time since 1927 to visit the exhibition. Paints a large triptych, *Study for Self-Portrait – Triptych*.

1988

Paints *Second Version of Triptych 1944*, exhibited as *Homage to Pierre Boulez* in Paris in April 1989. Exhibition at the Central House of Artists, New Tretyakov Gallery, Moscow.

1989–90

Numerous exhibitions held all over the world. Exhibition at Hirshhorn Museum and Sculpture Garden, Smithsonian Institution, Washington, subsequently shown in Los Angeles and New York. Exhibition at Marlborough Fine Art, London (1989).

1991

Paints *Study from the Human Body*.

1992

Goes to Madrid in the spring to visit friends. Feeling unwell, is taken to hospital, where he suffers a fatal heart attack. Dies on 28 April, at the age of eighty-two.

ONE-MAN EXHIBITIONS

1934

Transition Gallery, London.

1949

Hanover Gallery, London.

1950

Hanover Gallery, London.

1951–52

Hanover Gallery, London.

1952–53

Hanover Gallery, London.
Durlacher Brothers, New York.
Beaux Arts Gallery, London.

1954

British Pavilion, Venice Biennale.
Hanover Gallery, London.

1955

Institute of Contemporary Arts, London.
Hanover Gallery, London (with William Scott
and Graham Sutherland).

1957

Galerie Rive Droite, Paris.
Hanover Gallery, London.

1958

Galleria Galatea, Turin (afterwards at the
Galleria dell'Ariete, Milan, and L'Obelisco,
Rome).
Arts Council touring exhibition *Three Masters
of Modern British Painting* with Matthew Smith
and Victor Pasmore.

1959

Richard Feigen Gallery, Chicago.
Hanover Gallery, London.
V Bienal, São Paulo.

1960

Marlborough Fine Art, London.
University of California at Los Angeles (with
Hyman Bloom).

1961

Nottingham University, Nottingham.

1962–63

Retrospective at the Tate Gallery, London.
Modified versions of this exhibition were
afterwards shown at the Kunsthalle,
Mannheim: the Galleria Civica d'Arte
Moderna, Turin; the Kunsthaus, Zurich; and
(in 1963) at the Stedelijk Museum,
Amsterdam.
Galleria d'Arte Galatea, Milan.

1963–64

Retrospective at the Solomon R.
Guggenheim Museum, New York; afterwards
at the Art Institute of Chicago and the
Contemporary Art Association in Houston.
Galleria il Centro, Naples (with Graham
Sutherland).
Marlborough Fine Art, London.
Granville Gallery, New York.

1965

Retrospective at the Kunstverein, Hamburg;
afterwards at the Moderna Museet, Stockholm
and the Municipal Gallery of Modern Art,
Dublin.
Marlborough Fine Art, London.

1966

Galleria Toninelli, Milan.
Galerie Maeght, Paris.

1967

Galleria d'Arte Marlborough, Rome.
Galleria Toninelli, Milan.
Marlborough Fine Art, London.
Oberes Schloss, Siegen (Rubens Prize
Exhibition).

1968

Marlborough–Gerson Gallery, New York.

1970

Galleria d'Arte Galatea, Turin.

1971-72

Retrospective at the Grand Palais, Paris, and afterwards at the Kunsthalle, Düsseldorf.

1975

Metropolitan Museum of Art, New York.
Galerie Marlborough, Zurich.

1976

Musée Cantini, Marseille.

1977-78

Galerie Claude Bernard, Paris.
Museo de Arte Moderno, Mexico, and afterwards at the Museo de Arte Contemporáneo, Caracas.

1978

Fundácion Juan March, Madrid, and afterwards at the Fundació Joan Miró, Barcelona.

1980

Marlborough Gallery, New York.

1983

National Museum of Modern Art, Tokyo;
National Museum, Kyoto;
Aichi Prefectural Art Gallery, Nagoya.

1984

Galerie Maeght Lelong, Paris.
Marlborough Gallery, New York.
Thomas Gibson Fine Art, London.

1985-86

Retrospective at the Tate Gallery, London and afterwards at the Staatsgalerie, Stuttgart, and the Nationalgalerie, Berlin.
Marlborough Fine Art, London.

1987

Marlborough Gallery, New York.
Galerie Beyeler, Basel.
Galerie Lelong, Paris.

1988-89

Central House of Artists, New Tretyakov Gallery, Moscow.
Marlborough Fine Art, Tokyo.
Marlborough Fine Art, London.

1989-90

Hirshhorn Museum and Sculpture Garden, Smithsonian Institution, Washington D.C. Afterwards at the Los Angeles County Museum of Art, and the Museum of Modern Art, New York.
Marlborough Fine Art, London.
Marlborough Gallery, New York.

1990-91

Tate Gallery, Liverpool.

1992-93

Galeria Marlborough, Madrid and afterwards at the Marlborough Gallery, New York.
Museo d'Arte Moderna, Lugano.
Museo Correr, Venice.

1996-97

Centre Georges Pompidou, Paris and afterwards at the Haus der Kunst, Munich.

FILMOGRAPHY

Francis Bacon: Paintings 1944–1962, conceived and directed by David Thompson, with music by Elisabeth Lutyens. Made for the Arts Council of Great Britain and Marlborough Fine Art by Samaritan Films, London, 1962–63.

Sunday Night Francis Bacon: Interviews with David Sylvester, directed by Michael Gill for BBC Television, London, 1966.

Francis Bacon, interview with Maurice Chapuis, directed by J.-M. Berzosa, ORTF, Paris, 1971.

Portrait of Francis Bacon, directed by Thomas Ayck, NDR Television, Hamburg, 1974.

Interviews with Francis Bacon by David Sylvester, Aquarius, London Weekend Television, 1975.

Regards entendus Francis Bacon, text by Michel Leiris, produced by Constantin Jelenski, INA, 1983.

Après Hiroshima… Francis Bacon? Interview with Pierre Daix, ORTF, Paris, 1984.

The Brutality of Fact: Interview with David Sylvester, directed by Michael Blackwood and produced by Alan Yentob for *Arena,* BBC Television, London, 1984.

Francis Bacon, interview with Melvyn Bragg for *The South Bank Show,* London Weekend Television, 1985.

BIBLIOGRAPHY

Ades, Dawn and Andrew Forge, *Francis Bacon*, Thames and Hudson in association with the Tate Gallery, London, and Abrams, New York, 1985.

Alley, Ronald and Sir John Rothenstein, *Francis Bacon,* Thames and Hudson, London, and Viking Press, New York, 1964.

Archimbaud, Michel, *Francis Bacon in conversation with Michel Archimbaud*, Phaidon, London, 1993.

Davies, Hugh and Sally Yard, *Francis Bacon*, Abbeville Press, New York, 1986.

Deleuze, Gilles, *Francis Bacon: Logique de la Sensation*, 2 vols, Editions de la Différence, Paris, 1981; revised and corrected edition, 1984.

Dupin, Jacques, *Notes sur les dernières peintures*, Cahiers d'art contemporain, no. 39, Galerie Lelong, Paris, 1987.

Farson, Daniel, *The Gilded Gutter Life of Francis Bacon*, Century, London, 1993.

Francis Bacon, catalogue of the exhibition at the Grand Palais, Paris, 1971, and the Kunsthalle, Düsseldorf, 1972.

Francis Bacon, catalogue of the exhibition at the Museo d'Arte Moderna, Lugano, 1993.

Francis Bacon, catalogue of the exhibition at the Centre Georges Pompidou, Paris, 1996, and the Haus der Kunst, Munich, 1996–97.

Gowing, Lawrence and Sam Hunter, *Francis Bacon*, Thames and Hudson, London, in association with the Hirshhorn Museum and Sculpture Garden, Smithsonian Institution, Washington DC, 1989.

Leiris, Michel, *Francis Bacon, ou la vérité criante*, Fata Morgana/Scholies, Paris, 1974.

Leiris, Michel, *Francis Bacon, face et profil*, Albin Michel, Paris, 1983; *Francis Bacon: Full Face and in Profile,* tr. John Weightman, Phaidon, Oxford, and Rizzoli, New York, 1983.

Monsel, Philippe ed., *Bacon 1909–1992*, Cercle d'Art, Paris, 1994.

Rothenstein, Sir John, *Francis Bacon*, Fratelli Fabbri Editori, Milan, 1963, and Purnell, London, 1971.

Russell, John, *Francis Bacon*, Methuen, London, 1964.

Russell, John, *Francis Bacon*, Thames and Hudson, London, 1971; revised and updated editions 1979 and 1993.

Schmied, Wieland, *Francis Bacon: Vier Studien zu einem Porträt*, Frölich and Kaufmann, Berlin, 1985.

Sinclair Andrew, *Francis Bacon: His Life and Violent Times*, Sinclair-Stevenson, London, 1993.

Sollers, Philippe, *Francis Bacon*, Gallimard, Paris, 1996.

Sylvester, David, *Interviews with Francis Bacon*, Thames and Hudson, London, 1975; revised editions *Interviews with Francis Bacon 1962–1979*, 1980 and *The Brutality of Fact: Interviews with Francis Bacon*, 1987. Reprinted 1993 as *Interviews with Francis Bacon*.

Trucchi, Lorenza, *Francis Bacon*, Fratelli Fabbri Editori, Milan, 1975; tr. John Shepley, Thames and Hudson, London, 1976. (New revised edition, Fratelli Fabbri Editori, Milan, 1984.)

Zimmerman, Jörg, *Francis Bacon: Kreuzigung*, Fischer Taschenbuch, Frankfurt am Main, 1986.

LIST OF WORKS

Page 21
Portrait
c.1931–1932
Private Collection

Pages 22–25
*Three Studies for Portrait of George Dyer
(on light ground)*
1964
Private Collection

Page 26
Study for Head of George Dyer
1967
Private Collection

Page 27
Self-Portrait
1972
Private Collection

Pages 28–30
*Three Studies for Portrait of George Dyer
(on pink ground)*
1964
Private Collection

Page 31
Self-Portrait
1972
Private Collection

Pages 32–35
Three Studies of George Dyer
1966
Private Collection

Pages 36–39
Three Studies for Portrait of Isabel Rawsthorne
1965
Robert and Lisa Sainsbury Collection,
University of East Anglia, Norwich

Page 40
Study for Self-Portrait
1973
Private Collection

Pages 41–43
*Three Studies of Isabel Rawsthorne (on white
ground)*
1965
Private Collection

Pages 44–45
*Study for Head of Isabel Rawsthorne and George
Dyer*
1967
Private Collection

Pages 46–49
Three Studies for a Self-Portrait
1967
Private Collection

Page 50
Study for Head of Isabel Rawsthorne
1967
Private Collection

Pages 51–53
Three Studies of Isabel Rawsthorne
1968
Private Collection

Page 54
Study of Isabel Rawsthorne
1966
Musée National d'Art Moderne, Centre
Georges Pompidou, Paris, gift of Louise and
Michel Leiris

Pages 55–57
Studies of George Dyer and Isabel Rawsthorne
1970
Private Collection

Pages 58–60
Four Studies for a Self-Portrait
1967
Carlo Ponti

Page 61
Self-Portrait
1975
Private Collection

Page 62
Study for Head of Isabel Rawsthorne
1967
Private Collection

Page 63
Self-Portrait with Injured Eye
1972
Private Collection

Pages 64–67
Three Studies for Self-Portrait
1972
Private Collection

Pages 68–71
Three Studies of Isabel Rawsthorne (on light ground)
1965
Private Collection

Pages 72–73
Three Studies of Isabel Rawsthorne
1966
Private Collection

Pages 74–75
Two Studies for Self-Portrait
1977
Private Collection

Pages 76–79
Three Studies for Portraits: Isabel Rawsthorne, Lucian Freud and J. H.
1966
Private Collection

Pages 80–83
Three Studies for Portrait of Lucian Freud
1965
Marlborough International Fine Art

Page 84
Portrait of Lucian Freud
1965
Private Collection

Page 86
Study for Head of Lucian Freud
1967
Private Collection

Page 87
Self-Portrait
1973
Private Collection

Page 88
Portrait of Man with Glasses III
1963
Private Collection

Page 89
Self-Portrait
1972
Private Collection

Pages 90–91
Three Studies for Self-Portrait
1974
Private Collection

Pages 92–94
Three Studies for Self-Portrait
1976
Private Collection

Pages 95–97
Triptych
1977
Private Collection

Pages 98–100
Head II and Head IV
1961
Private Collection

Page 101
Head III
1961
Private Collection

Pages 102–105
Three Studies of Muriel Belcher
1966
Private Collection

Page 106
Self-Portrait
1969
Private Collection

Page 107
Self-Portrait
1972
Private Collection

Page 108
Henrietta Moraes
1969
Private Collection

Pages 109–111
Two Studies for Self-Portrait
1972
Private Collection

Pages 112–115
Three Studies of Henrietta Moraes
1969
Private Collection

Page 116
Self-Portrait
1969
Private Collection

Pages 117–120
Three Studies of Henrietta Moraes
1969
Massimo Martino S.A., Lugano

Pages 121–123
Three Studies for Portrait of Henrietta Moraes
1963
Museum of Modern Art, New York,
William S. Paley Collection

Pages 124–125
Study of Henrietta Moraes Laughing
1969
Private Collection

Page 126
Self-Portrait
1971
Musée National d'Art Moderne, Centre
Georges Pompidou, Paris, gift of Louise
and Michel Leiris

Pages 127–129
Three Studies for a Portrait (Mick Jagger)
1982
Private Collection

Pages 130–133
Three Studies for a Portrait of Peter Beard
1975
Private Collection

Pages 134–137
Three Studies for Self-Portrait
1980
Private Collection

Page 138
Study for a Portrait
1978
Private Collection

Page 139
Self-Portrait
1976
Musée Cantini, Marseille

Pages 140–143
Three Studies for Self-Portrait
1979
The Metropolitan Museum of Art, New
York, Jacques and Natasha Gelman Collection

Page 144
Study for Self-Portrait
1978
Private Collection

Page 145
Study for Self-Portrait
1979
Private Collection

Pages 146–148
Three Studies for a Portrait (Peter Beard)
1980
Marlborough International Fine Art

Pages 149–152
Three Studies for a Portrait (Peter Beard)
1975
Private Collection

Page 153
Portrait of Jacques Dupin
1990
FNAC (on loan to the Musée de Picardie,
Amiens)

Page 155
Study for Portrait (Michel Leiris)
1978
Musée National d'Art Moderne, Centre
Georges Pompidou, Paris, gift of Louise
and Michel Leiris

Page 156
Portrait of Michel Leiris
1976
Musée National d'Art Moderne, Centre
Georges Pompidou, Paris, gift of Louise
and Michel Leiris

Pages 157–160
Three Studies for Portraits including Self-Portrait
1969
Private Collection

Pages 161–163
Three Studies for Self-Portrait
1983
Honolulu Academy of Arts, gift of Mr and
Mrs Henry B. Clark Jr

Page 164
Study for Self-Portrait
1980
Private Collection

Page 165
Self-Portrait
1987
Private Collection

Pages 166–168
Two Studies for Portrait of Richard Chopping
1978
Private Collection

Page 169
Study for Portrait of John Edwards
1989
Private Collection

Page 170
Study for Portrait of John Edwards
1989
Simon Spierer, Geneva

Pages 172–175
Three Studies for Self-Portrait
1973
Private Collection

Pages 176–179
Study for Three Heads
1962
The Museum of Modern Art, New York,
William S. Paley Collection

Pages 180–181
Two Studies for a Self-Portrait
1970
Private Collection

Photographs: © The Estate of Francis Bacon

ACKNOWLEDGMENTS

The publishers would like to thank the Estate of Francis Bacon, Valerie Beston and Kate Austin of Marlborough Fine Art, London, and Michel Desgranges, Yves Le Houerf and Martine Reyss.